O9-ABF-656

Growing
Up Again

Also by Mary Tyler Moore

After All

Growing Up Again

Life, Loves, and Oh Yeah, Diabetes

Mary Tyler Moore

St. Martin's Press  New York

GROWING UP AGAIN. Copyright © 2009 by Mary Tyler Moore. All rights reserved. Printed in the United States of America. For information, address St. Martin's Press, 175 Fifth Avenue, New York, N.Y. 10010.

www.stmartins.com

Design by Rich Arnold

"The Nest of a Hawk" used with permission. Copyright © 2004 by Matthew Sperling.

Library of Congress Cataloging-in-Publication Data

Moore, Mary Tyler, 1936–
    Growing up again : life, loves, and oh yeah, diabetes / Mary Tyler Moore. — 1st ed.
    p. cm.
    ISBN-13: 978-0-312-37631-4
    ISBN-10: 0-312-37631-6
    1. Moore, Mary Tyler, 1936—Health.   2. Diabetics—United States—Biography.
3. Actresses—United States—Biography.   I. Title.
    RC660.4.M66 2009
    362.196′4620092—dc22
    [B]
                                           2008037579

First Edition: April 2009

10 9 8 7 6 5 4 3 2 1

For Robert, my younger suitor, who has lovingly nudged me to poke around the dusty attic at my leisure for more clues in putting this character together

Contents

Diabetes Resource Guide

Index

Acknowledgments

My deepest gratitude to the brilliant scientists who contributed to this book and who, while improving our lives, search so fiercely for the cure.

Phil Revzin, St. Martin's Press senior editor, has nobly served that good office while looking out for his favorite "kid sister." Thank you, Phil.

Karen Brownlee, Director of Foundation Relations for the Juvenile Diabetes Research Foundation, has so wisely guided my efforts on their behalf these past twenty-four years, including with my writing of this book. I thank you, dear friend.

With fond thanks to Kalia Doner for always maintaining a brave smile, even when my muse seemed more moose-like than inspiring.

"Uncle Tee" Sims, your help in putting this book together— with the Internet, typing, occasional suggestions—makes you my best friend. I love for you for that, too.

> Dear Diane Revzin,
> Thank you for your kind invitation.
> I had a very good time.
> > Sincerely,
> > MTM

Preface

This book has been one of the most exciting projects of my life. It came about at the behest of a lovely young woman named Diane Revzin, age nineteen, who is the daughter of Philip Revzin, senior editor at St. Martin's Press. She has type 1 diabetes.

It seems that one day father and daughter were washing the family car—an enjoyable weekend task Diane thought of as a kind of sporting event the two of them could share. "How's it going?" her dad asked.

"Oh, you know, okay, I guess," she replied, but then tossed down her sponge (a most unusual attitude for her) and blurted out, "I wish I had a diabetic best friend, someone to talk to about what it's like to have diabetes. Sometimes I feel, I don't know, alone. Ya know?"

Her father lowered his head and looked at her over the rims of his glasses and answered, "Honey, you're as well informed as anybody, having read most of the books out there."

"But I want to know about someone else's experiences with diabetes. You're right, I've pretty much read the 'ABC's of Diabetes' and the 'What to Do' books. I want to read someone else's personal experiences, both good and bad, and the emotional gymnastics that go with it all. Is there anybody like that you can think of, Dad?"

Dear Phil thought of me! He tells me he set out my diabetes bio for Diane's consideration—"Mary Tyler Moore. She's a diabetic, first and foremost; she's the international chairman of the Juvenile Diabetes Research Foundation [JDRF]; and she makes me laugh. I kind of think that's important. She seems to be deeply involved in the government relations for JDRF, including the time she spends in Washington lobbying Congress for increases in federal funding for research."

"I know she can't be my buddy," Diane replied, "but maybe she can come up with something."

When Phil called me, I was in the last throes of unpacking an endless array of clothes, beauty products (I keep trying), medications, toiletries, and diabetes lifelines: insulin (two types), syringes, monitors, test tapes, charts, list of appropriate insulin doses, test strips used to spot the dreaded ketones in urine, glucose tablets, alcohol swabs, a glucagon emergency kit, lancets, diabetes literature, stacks and stacks of books and letters on the subject, and a box of chocolate-covered raisins.

My husband, Robert, and I were carrying out the decision we'd made to move out of our apartment in Manhattan to live full-time at our country house in Millbrook, New York. It was a major upheaval, but we had strong longings for open skies, riding trails, meadows, animals, and the quiet.

It was my cell phone. It was there, somewhere. I could hear it screaming at me! I ought to give myself a break and change to nicer, less critical music. But then I might never find it.

Aha! There it was, the phone, buried under some exercise leotards. I plucked the damn thing out of the jumbled mess of (would-be) ballerina togs, grateful for the opportunity to sit, and offered my all-purpose, if a bit breathless, "Hello."

"May I speak to Mary Tyler Moore?" a male voice asked.

And in a most proper tone (Dad would be proud) I answered, "This is she." (It sometimes takes guts to be correct with our language. I now opt for the compromise of "Speaking.")

With a smile in his voice, my "gentleman caller" said, "I'm Phil Revzin—St. Martin's Press. We'd like to talk to you about writing a book concerning your experiences with diabetes. I'll speak to your agent, of course, but before I do that, I'd like to know if the idea is of some interest to you."

Hmmm.

And that's how it began.

Growing
Up Again

1

Sotto Voce

Chronic disease, like a troublesome relative, is something you can learn to manage but never quite escape. And while each and every person who has type 1 prays for a cure, and would give anything to stop thinking about it for just a year, a month, a week, a day even, the ironic truth is that only when you own it—accept it, embrace it, make it your own—do you start to be free of many of its emotional and physical burdens.

How do you accomplish this acceptance? How do you come to terms with this constant, nagging, never-ending disease? I can't tell you, not precisely. Each person who has diabetes struggles to come to terms with it and experiences the basic challenges of the disease in a uniquely personal way. For me, it has been a trip through rebellion and denial to finally arriving at acknowledgment and commitment to solutions. It took years. And the restrictions, the have-tos, the may-nots, and the never-endingness of it still rankle. But the illness is what it is, and I thank God for the genius of medical researchers, who have done so much to make diabetes a less cruel imposition while propelling us toward a cure.

I don't think the story of my life with diabetes is a model

for anyone else. There's no template to follow that will determine the course of the disease and how it affects a person's life; no one right way to manage diabetes. What I have put on paper is simply the tale of how, in the course of everyday living—dealing with the losses, the dead ends, and the triumphs that come in often seemingly random order—I've dodged, faced, and sometimes conquered the challenges of diabetes. I'm sharing my story because it is what I have to give, shedding some light on the follies and achievements that I've racked up in my daily confrontation with the disease.

But my journey is just a part of the picture. So I've talked with other people who have diabetes to give voice to their experiences, to provide a varied view of how to live and thrive. And I've sought out some of the wisest and most capable doctors and scientists who are waging war in the laboratory and conducting bench-to-bedside experiments that are producing new and exciting treatments to help the millions of people with diabetes manage—and ultimately vanquish—the disease. A lot of this practical information appears in the appendixes at the back of the book.

It is my most heartfelt hope that the collective wisdom— and occasional humor—of the stories contained herein will help others who have diabetes, and their loved ones, find new ways of managing its challenges.

For me, the process of writing the book, talking with people with diabetes and all the experts, certainly has provided new insights into how to manage the disease. I guess you could say it truly has been a matter of growing up again. So let me introduce myself one more time. . . .

2

The Other Shoe Falls . . . and Falls and Falls

I'm Mary Tyler Moore and I am . . . an actress, an animal lover, the chairman of the Juvenile Diabetes Research Foundation, the wife of Dr. Robert Levine, and . . . I don't want to give away the whole story from the very start. Suffice it to say there are a lot of ways to end that sentence, and I don't think I've come close to living through all the possibilities, thank heavens. But what I do know is that in every role I am a devotee of laughter and tears, committed to expressing the nuances of each.

For our purposes here, though, I am going to write about who I am in relation to diabetes. I'll start in 1969, the year I was diagnosed with type 1. It was a time of transition for me: It was three years after *The Dick Van Dyke Show* had ended. That show had catapulted me from a nervous chorus girl from Studio City, California, to a famous actress (quite a head-spinner and life-changer). And it was a year before *The Mary Tyler Moore Show* debuted.

In that interim period, Dick was kind enough to ask me to join him in a television special called "Dick Van Dyke and the Other Woman," warmly spoofing the couple we had played on *The Dick Van Dyke Show,* Rob and Laura Petrie, and their marriage, with which the public had become so very smitten. Little did I know at the time that the special was to be the launching pad for my future—my career, my loves, my disappointments, heartbreaks, challenges, and successes. Thanks to Dick's genius and his generosity in sharing the spotlight with me, the show was a great hit. And afterward CBS asked me to think about what I'd like to do in a series of my own! Wow, really? Oh, thank you, God, thank you! Thank you, Dick!

My second husband, Grant Tinker, a successful network vice president whom I'd married in 1963, left his post to become the King of Camelot, MTM Enterprises, which produced some thirty pilots and series over a dozen years, many winning multiple Emmys and the praise of critics as well. Of these shows, mine was the first. Thank you, Grant, thank you!

But despite, or maybe because of, the thrill of our accomplishments together, I realized later that I had not been captain of my own ship—not even co-captain. I see now that it was a pattern that had long manifested itself in my personal relationships, my working life, my early marriages.

I married for the first time right out of high school, leaving the complicated but protective, even totalitarian, environment of my parents' unstable home for the adventure of "wifedom" and motherhood. I was eighteen, my husband was the very kind twenty-eight-year-old boy next door, Richard Meeker. And since he had a job (cranberry sauce sales manager) and his own apartment (as I said, next door), I accepted the invitation to get married on the condition that we move at least four blocks away from my parents. Now that was an independent step, wasn't it?

I had just graduated from Immaculate Heart High School in Hollywood, California, and had no preparation for real life. I didn't even type! That was because, as I entered high school, my mother said, "Be sure you take a typing course in case this show business thing doesn't work out." Thanks for the vote of confidence, Mother! Watch me never take your advice!

How sorry I am now that I let her understandable disbelief in my not-so-promising future influence me long past the "I'll show you!" stage. As I write this book in longhand on yellow lined paper that contains erasures, cross-outs, and indecipherable smudges, I look longingly at my assistant and dear friend, Terry Sims, typing away on his computer and I wish for a "do-over" of that resentment.

Less than a year after I married Richard, I gave birth to a 9-pound, 3½-ounce boy, whom we named Richard. We formed a family, and for the next five years I was working when I could land a role on a television show or a job as a chorus dancer. All the while, I put meals on the table, cooed and rocked, cleaned, and chatted with other moms in the park. I was cared for, and I was the best mom I knew how to be. When that marriage ended, I landed the role on *The Dick Van Dyke Show*; proudly I realized that I could take care of Richie and myself, at least economically. But emotionally I was not ready to take the helm and be the captain of the HMS *Mary Tyler Moore*. A few years later, in 1962, I married Grant.

Grant was unique in many ways, yet so recognizable to me as the protective alpha dog. Once again, a familiar and comforting mantle of safety draped itself around my shoulders, allowing me to express myself as an actress but making it necessary for me to take charge of little else.

It would be wrong for me to insinuate that I was forced into some kind of servitude. I did it to myself, inadvertently, as a diva in the making, perhaps? While I never felt the need to make anyone's life diva-difficult, I did feel it was appropriate for a man (father) to assume the role of decision maker, the one who took over when I was unable to, or disinterested in, taking the reins.

It felt right as an adult to have this captain's chair occupied by an intelligent, fiercely witty man, Grant, whose focus was to become the building of MTM Enterprises, Inc., including the care of its flagship, *The Mary Tyler Moore Show.* And, come on, let's be fair to me: Wasn't my contribution that I was free to help create the earnest, lovable Mary Richards, who, after all, was a major asset in the business that was "show"?

I was a mother, too, requiring no small amount of self, which kept me very busy being loving, organized about time spent together, and just hanging out. While I had the best of intentions and high hopes, I did, I think, miss out on some of the perks of motherhood, such as spending time in the park on a random afternoon, or sitting on the living room floor together playing checkers. While Richie was young, I did two series, *The Dick Van Dyke Show* and *The Mary Tyler Moore Show.* And truth be told, work was my focus before, during, and after. If I had it to do over, I wouldn't have pursued a career while I had a little boy to care for. My heart breaks when I think of the times missed, times with him. How predictable that without awareness I emulated my mother's behavior toward me.

But before I figured all that out I sailed through the process of launching the show, astounded and delighted by the creativity that surrounded me.

As we were preparing to do the series, a surprise pregnancy gave the promise of a huge event. Since the show wasn't due to air for almost a year, it was accidentally, yet exquisitely, timed. So, Grant and I set about the fun of telling anyone who'd listen that we were embarking on a production of another sort.

In about six weeks' time the promise was broken. This growing expression of us both ended in its beginning. And the loss took my heart with it as well. Later that day my physicians entered the hospital room with that look doctors get when there's bad news (as noted on television). It seems that during the necessary D&C procedure that followed the miscarriage, it was discovered that there might be a little problem with the amount of sugar present in my blood. The normal count is between 70 and 110. Mine was 750!

"Mrs. Tinker," my doctor intoned, "It looks like you may have"—cue the drumroll!—"juvenile diabetes." I thought, Juvenile? *Diabetes?!* What?!—I'm not that childish! And I am not that special!

I can't believe I thought the diagnosis made me special. But I did and I couldn't wait to share the exciting news with everyone. Ah, such thoughts revealed my stunning insecurity in slightly loopy ways. There I was, a multiple Emmy Award winner, dozens of times on the cover of *TV Guide,* a darling of the critics, and I needed a major disease to make me feel whole? Let's chalk it up to films that had a strong influence on me from way back when they were called movies: the wheelchair-bound little girl who won Heidi's love and attention; Deborah Kerr, who waited to be reunited with Cary Grant after she lost the use of her legs in a terrible car crash; and, of course, Camille, whose imminent death ripped the hearts from so many. All of these, plus a few more, made me believe in the magical power of illness to elicit love. Seemed like a good thing to me!

"Did you have a lot of cake last night for dessert?" the doctor asked. (I thought this was a bit cheeky.)

No, I huffed.

"Do you know anything about diabetes?"

A little (the one question I lied about). I knew diabetes was one of the big ones on the major diseases chart. But my knowledge of it measured . . . zip! In fact, I vaguely thought it condemned one to a lifetime of eating chocolates while reclining on a chaise, resting, never to dance again. I have no idea why I thought this!

"Have you been feeling tired? What about urination—any more than usual? Are you always thirsty and dry in the mouth?"

No, not really—and no.

I noticed that some of the medical professionals who had been called to my bedside seemed a bit confused; there was a lot of head-scratching going on. They were stunned that I had been walking around without feeling any symptoms of diabetes with such a high blood-glucose level. In retrospect, I had noticed a few oddities, but I had chalked them up to the pregnancy. I'd had a feeling of fatigue upon reaching the top of the stairs in our house. And instead of attempting an Astaire-like flourish at the summit, I'd been unable to do anything but grasp the top of the banister and breathe, simply breathe.

When engaging in conversations, my mouth would become dry sometimes, so much so that I wondered if the person I was talking to could hear the clicking sounds I made as my tongue (starved for moisture) would smack against my teeth. I began keeping a bottle of water handy, and berry teas became my only harmless addiction. Not knowing better at that time, I smoked and drank. Maybe those indulgences were a factor in the miscarriage? The planning of *The Mary Tyler Moore show* was happily stressful, and I'm sure that added to my distraction, as well.

But in thinking about this inability to notice the symptoms of diabetes, I've come up with a couple of insights. The first possible answer is a paradox. You might assume that a trained dancer—me—would be tuned in to her body during a performance and during everyday life. But a crucial requirement to be a dancer is an ability to ignore the never-far-away physical pain that accompanies both the long-term training and moments of performance. Ah, yes, the performance, during which the face, at all times, must reflect nothing but the expression of the character one is portraying. The toes may be bleeding, calf muscles screaming, but never, ever acknowledge it! We dancers, make no mistake, are like football players. We play with pain. So, I think admitting to fatigue or discomfort goes against what was, by that time, my nature.

The other truth? I drank consistently every evening at six o'clock for many years. Could that have dulled my senses? You bet! Grant and I were feeling carefree, high-spirited, and dulled at the same time.

So diabetes arrived as a surprise—denied before diagnosis and marginalized after.

It wasn't that I didn't want to take good care of myself, but it was just not that easy to do in those days. And I didn't know enough to ask for the kind of support and help that might have made managing it easier and more successful. As I've said, I wasn't about to captain my own ship, even if my health depended on it.

The doctors hoped (mistakenly) that I would become an expert planner and keeper of records. But this, mind you, was supposed to be done without the benefit of blood testing at home. In those days, one had to rely on passing a test strip through a stream of urine three or four times daily to find out what the glucose levels were. This method was inaccurate at best. The only readings (as I perceived them) from this testing were +1 (excellent), +2 (you can do better), +3 (you'll be sorry), and +4 (you are a complete failure!). Finger sticks in search of blood were to come some twenty years later. There was only one type of insulin.

I don't mean to complain. Other friends of mine who were diagnosed even longer ago than I have really hair-raising memories of trying to manage their diabetes. John McDonough, a dynamo who has had diabetes for more than six decades, has scaled the peaks of corporate success, had one leg amputated below the knee, and now runs one of the most advanced (and charitable) prosthetic device companies in the world. He has battled his way to a long, full life. Over the years we've talked a lot about the Juvenile Diabetes Research Foundation (he was chairman of the international board), families, life's little bumps and rewards, but I don't think I ever really knew just how tough his childhood had been until we sat down together one day over diet Cokes. John told me his paternal grandfather had died in 1912 of the complications of diabetes and that made his own diagnosis terrifying to his father.

"When I was diagnosed sixty-six years ago, I was six years

old," he said. "My poor father was devastated. But my mother, who was of Norwegian descent, was really tough. I was not allowed to think I had problems. I would be out in back playing basketball and start to go a little low and my mother would bring me juice. But she wouldn't allow me in the house. I had to go back into the game.

"As for managing glucose levels—that was all done with food and exercise. My mother would weigh the food, and I would eat everything on the plate whether I liked it or not. If I didn't do something right she would crack me with my father's razor strop. And then she said if I told my father she would crack me twice. But she saved my life over and over again. Marilyn, my wife of fifty-one years, has done the same many, many times.

"At that time all you would do was go to the hospital every three or four months to be evaluated. And I would need a new insulin regimen to accommodate my growth spurts. I took just one shot a day.

"It was difficult—my childhood. My mother wasn't just frugal, she was cheap. She would use the same needle for a very long time—kept it in a jug of alcohol. She would file it. And it would eventually be so dull that it could barely break the skin. I complained and she said, 'If you think you can do it better, do it yourself.' And from that day on I did it myself. I learned to give myself a shot when I was eight years old.

"But for all I'd been through, nothing hit me as hard as when my daughter Allison was diagnosed at age twenty-four. She was working with me and was very worn out. But we just thought she had been working too hard. Then one day I saw her drinking enough water to drain Lake Michigan. I said, 'Come with me,' and we did a blood test. Her sugar was sky-high. It was the start of an emotional roller coaster.

"At first I thought, Why did this happen to me? Why me, God? And then I had a good long cry. I thought, I did this to her. She was the first of our five children. I did this to her. And then finally I said to myself, 'Enough. We have this problem. What are we going to do? What do *we* have to do in order to make it better?' Obviously, all I could do was improve my own control to set an example for her. And over the years, she has done the same. I am sure that because of this we have both added some years to our lives."

When I was diagnosed, my own version of John's acquired wisdom was years away. I was still trying to figure out what had happened to me—and so were the doctors.

Shortly after I was told I had diabetes, I overheard some discussions among the interns who visited me about whether the pregnancy and ultimate miscarriage were the triggers for diabetes or did the diabetes kill the pregnancy? The uncertainty of cause and effect haunted me—could I have done something to prevent the miscarriage? To prevent the diabetes? There were no answers. Now, as we'll talk about later, they know that diabetes takes years to develop, and one incident, such as a miscarriage, is not necessarily the only or the immediate cause.

I remained under the microscope for a few days while doctors and nurses did their best to teach me what, how much, and when to eat, the intricacies of loading a syringe with insulin and injecting it into my own flesh (oh, come on—aren't there nurses to do that?), and how to time the insulin injections to take place exactly one half hour before meals.

After learning as much as I could digest about my new life sentence, I was sent home from the hospital with all manner of prizes—charts, graphs, a daily journal, and urine-testing strips. What a responsibility I had now become to myself. My head was spinning. And, boy, was I scared! What if I messed up filling the syringe? In removing fluid from a vial, it is necessary to inject an equal amount of air before withdrawing the insulin. Often, it creates an air bubble in the syringe, which can be removed by tapping on it, then withdrawing a little bit more air and expelling it before the injection. What if I wasn't as careful as I should be? I could inject that air bubble into an artery, which would carry it straight to my brain . . . or would it be my heart? I'd forgotten to ask that, of course. (Everybody worries about this at first, but luckily it's not a problem, because the short little needles used for insulin go into the flesh, not a vein, and there's no danger of injecting a lethal air bubble.)

I tried to get over my mental block by practicing on prized California oranges. Even that was frightening to me. I'd hold the orange in my left hand, as my right hand—trembling, but sincerely aiming—held the syringe. I was an excellent aimer, if nothing else—stab the air/retreat, stab/retreat, and again stab/retreat, without once piercing the orange's skin.

I look back on those first months (and years) remembering the fear and nausea I felt at the thought of injecting myself, and I wonder how I managed to keep it together through all the rehearsals and filming of *The Mary Tyler Moore Show* and our busy public life.

I must say I did a remarkable job of it—but there were a few blips along the way.

One that stands out in my memory happened during one of our Monday-morning meetings, when the cast would assemble to read through that week's script. On this particular Monday we had a guest director, so this was an important opportunity to get to know one another as we found the jokes and added to them, as well. I'd felt a bit jittery as I'd driven to work, but I didn't know what could account for it. Certainly I wasn't nervous about meeting the new director (well, yes, a bit); certainly I hadn't had too much coffee (well, perhaps); certainly I had had enough to eat (well, I was on a diet to lose a few pounds gained on vacation and was familiar with the vague light-headedness that goes along with hunger). But the truth was, I was relatively new to the signs of the carnival ride awaiting me. So that morning, unbeknownst to me, I was being swept off my feet by hypoglycemia—low blood sugar.

Hypoglycemia—a blood sugar level of 70 or less—can happen to people with type 1 diabetes if our meals or snacks are too small, delayed, or skipped; if we take too much insulin; if we have increased our level of physical activity or exercise without decreasing our medications appropriately; or if we have type 2 and are taking some oral diabetes medications. Usually hypoglycemia can be treated by eating or drinking something rich with carbohydrates, such as orange juice or candy or, in a crisis, taking an injection of a specially prepared super-charged blood-sugar elevator, glucagon. Left untreated, hypoglycemia can lead to loss of consciousness; and while you're still wobbling around, trying to get ahold of your body and emotions, it feels unbelievably horrible—like you are losing your mind, if you have one left to lose.

As the cast and crew introduced themselves to the new guy, I felt my voice wavering. I remember the unsure faces of my dear friends as they tried to make sense of the apparition who used to be Mary. I began crying while trying to explain what it was: "It's my diabetes. No, my diet. I didn't recognize it. It's not your fault." I jabbered on in an attempt to will the now-terrifying feeling away.

At some point our producer, Allan Burns, grabbed my hair, pulled my head back, and began to pour orange juice down my throat. He'd had the presence of mind to call my doctor. It worked. In ten minutes I could feel myself returning to normal.

After that, the week went well and the new director seemed pleased with the results. Only years later did I find out that our guest "helmer" had indeed enjoyed the week, though he was on pins and needles worrying about Mary, "who was apparently addicted to diet pills"! Thank God that falsehood didn't take flight!

On learning of the event, Cloris Leachman's response was, "Why the hell were you on a diet? And what does diabetes have to do with acting so strangely anyway?!"

And so I began again, trying to explain.

Defining Diabetes

Type 1, or juvenile, diabetes, so named because it usually strikes youngsters (I was a youthful thirty-three), is a disease that causes the body to launch an immune system attack on its own insulin-producing beta cells in the pancreas.

The pancreas sits behind the lower part of the stomach. This palm-sized organ contains clusters of cells called islets. They, in turn, are made up of several types of cells, including beta cells—and that's where insulin is produced. Insulin is a hormone that measures the carbohydrates you've eaten and is automatically released to moderate the glucose-raising effects of those carbs on the bloodstream.

In type I diabetes, that process fails when the immune system has killed off so many beta cells that there are not enough remaining to provide sufficient insulin, and blood glucose levels soar unchecked. Over time, elevated glucose levels and other changes in body chemistry (inflammation, for example) may trigger a whole roster of diabetes-related complications—heart disease, kidney problems, nerve damage, and diabetic eye disease (retinopathy) are the major disorders. We'll look into my experiences with eye problems later.

But what causes the disease?

If I had the answer to that I'd have a Nobel Prize! What I do have, however, is the opportunity to talk with some amazing scientists who are willing to share their insights and knowledge. So I can tell you that the current scientific consensus is that type I diabetes is brought on by the combination of a genetic predisposition (turns out there are many, many genes that may play a role, singly or in combination) and environmental triggers, such as a virus or a chemical, as well as other biochemical activities in the body that are yet to be fully identified. And it seems to me that combination of genes plus physical and emotional trauma preceded my diagnosis.

The researchers know genes are not the whole story, because if one identical twin gets diabetes before the age of six, the other has about a 60 percent chance of also being diagnosed; if one twin is diagnosed after the age of twenty-five then the risk to the other twin falls to only about 6 percent. Not so identical, in either case. And as for the environmental trigger, well, to borrow a phrase from Mark Atkinson, Ph.D., of the University of Florida's Departments of Pathology and Pediatrics and a lead researcher in many of the JDRF-funded efforts seeking a better understanding of why the disease develops, the "list seems to grow every couple of months and it's already longer than your arm." The truth is, we don't yet fully understand what causes type 1 because so many different triggers may be involved.

So, I asked Dr. Atkinson, "When do the triggers that cause type 1 diabetes strike?"

He explained that no matter if you are diagnosed at the age of three or thirty, it appears that the process of developing the disease likely starts early—in the first fifteen to twenty-four months of life. "And we now know, as your particular case clearly demonstrates, that it can take months to years or even decades for full-blown type 1 to develop," he told me. "Despite remarkable advances in researchers' ability to predict who is at increased risk for developing type 1, it remains a little unpredictable when it comes to saying exactly who will get the disease and when it will occur."

But what we do know for sure—and I know firsthand—is that once type 1 is diagnosed you have to be thoughtful about what you eat, when you eat, and how you take your insulin. All the science in the world doesn't change the fact that if that goes awry, your blood sugar levels can hit highs and lows that affect not only your long-term health but how you feel and function at that moment.

All this information adds up to me, sitting around the conference table before the filming of a *Mary Tyler Moore Show* episode, babbling at our guest director because for a set of unknown reasons my body could no longer regulate blood sugar levels on its own. And if I mess up—as I did by skipping breakfast that morning but still taking my insulin—well, welcome to the wonderful Technicolor world of hypoglycemia!

So there you have my answer to Cloris's question "What does diabetes have to do with acting so strangely?"

Taking It in Stride

I'm not telling you anything you don't know when I say that managing diabetes is a big job. But I've been told it multiple times (maybe a thousand!) by doctors and friends and husbands (well, at least one: Robert), and I still need to hear it to help me stay on top of it all and not get discouraged or frustrated. And then—because I am singularly stubborn, even when it is not to my own advantage—sometimes I just walk away from it all and stop being careful about what I eat, or when I test. So here's the drill. And I am paying attention, really I am.

First, you need to spend a good deal of time calculating the amount of carbohydrates you have eaten and the right amount of insulin to inject in compensation. And you start testing your blood sugars three or four times a day to make sure you are on track to "normal." Too high or too low is, over time, courting medical disaster.

I can now see (isn't hindsight glorious?!) that the real importance of all this escaped me when I was first diagnosed. It just made me so angry to have to live by another set of rules and regulations.

When I got home from the hospital and walked into the kitchen, I found that our concerned housekeeper and Grant had thrown out or given away everything that tasted any good at all. No cookies (not even a graham cracker). No sugared cereals. Even orange juice was no longer smiling at me when I opened the refrigerator door. I was told, however, that only on those hopefully rare occasions when my sugar level had proven to be too low, I would be adjusting it by drinking orange juice, just so much—four ounces. "Well, how very kind of you! Aren't I the lucky one!" So I got in my car and drove to the market, where I bought a dozen glazed doughnuts and ate every one of them (well, most of them) while driving home. Fifteen glorious minutes of self-delusion. I was able to make the facts all go away during that mobile sugar festival. What an angry child I'd become.

One of the terrible things about diabetes (and there are many terrible things about it) is that it can be deceptive, leading some to think it might be played with—that you can depart from the recommended routine. Most of the time, when my blood sugar is high, I feel only minor discomfort. It isn't until later that the pay-up comes due. When I eat as I did that day, I don't double over with pain or gasp for air. I feel fine until my system, having no way to process those carbohydrates with which I've gagged it, breaks down, unable to direct the sugar to where it should be—in the cells of my body. Then, I feel even drier in the mouth, hot all over, and weak. In those days of peeing on the test strip, facing the inevitable +4 readout was the worst symptom of all, nearly destroying my fragile self-esteem.

Fortunately, things have changed since then. My attitude is somewhat better, and I have graduated from bingeing on doughnuts to the judicious indulgence, on rare occasions (am I telling the truth?), in the creamy lusciousness of tiramisù. There is a wonderful variety of insulins that work to compensate for what I may eat. It's easier to keep tabs on my blood sugar levels. And there is the relatively new way to track glucose levels over time—the A1C, or glycosylated hemoglobin test. It measures your average blood sugar level from the previous two- to three-month period—an excellent method for your doctor to see how much reevaluating needs to be done on your food and insulin intake and exercise output. There is even an at-home version for those who like to do such tests themselves. One caveat: This is no substitute for multiple daily glucose monitoring.

Dr. William Tamborlane, director of the Yale University Children's Diabetes Program and chief of pediatric endocrinology, and one of the developers of the insulin pump, believes that one of the best things a parent can do for a diabetic child is to find a doctor who can do the quarterly test in the office and get on-the-spot results. "I tell my patients that their main task is to keep their eye on the target—a good A1C level of six or seven," he told me recently. "And having the test results right there in the office, well, it's like a quarterly report card and kids can really attach meaning to the results."

Let me tell you: so can adults. Sometimes my AIC's are higher than I expect and I feel a rush of guilt and anger—which does nothing, of course, to right the glucose levels or to change my uneasy relationship to managing this disease.

The Upside of Down

For young people and their parents, a diagnosis of diabetes can be earthshaking. But when they join forces and work together to understand how to integrate diabetes management into everyday life, it's amazing how—I hesitate to say it, but it's true—how positive an experience it can turn out to be. It shapes a child's view of the world and themselves in interesting ways—creates compassion, responsibility, generosity of spirit, appreciation of every day. That's what I have seen in the kids I talk with year after year across the country. But I'll let you judge for yourself.

To get a sense of what life with diabetes seems like from a youngster's point of view, some remarkable kids who have been living with diabetes for most of their lives plopped themselves down around a conference table at JDRF headquarters one day. With an openness and humor that took me by surprise, they gave me an insider's tour. Two of them, Samantha Mandel, seventeen, and Matt Rodriguez, thirteen—so different in ages, backgrounds, and temperaments—had the strongest points of view about what being diabetic meant to their lives.

Samantha, who was about to start college, sat across from me. She worked with JDRF as a delegate for the Children's Congress in 1999 and as an intern at the New York City chapter in the summer of 2006. She is adamant: "I have had diabetes since two weeks after my second birthday. It's made me the person I am. It gives me a sense of responsibility and independence. You become mature because you have to think about your decisions—cause and effect. It's no longer, 'I am a person with diabetes.' I am a diabetic."

Matt, wise beyond his years, has an intensity and energy that make him seem like he's always in motion. He's turned the difficulties, physical and psychological, of having diabetes into fuel for creative action. "Without diabetes my life would have been totally different. I was four years old when I was diagnosed. We were in Florida, the day before we were supposed to go to Disney World. I had all kinds of symptoms, so my mom called the pediatrician and she said to go to the hospital right away. That was it. It changed everything. Without diabetes, I would have lived somewhere else, had totally different friends; my parents and sister would be totally different. I'd have a totally different attitude. A whole lot of things that happened in my life revolve around diabetes. I have gotten awards because of diabetes. Without diabetes I wouldn't have done the community service I have done now—I started a whole program that supplies baseball cleats to kids in the Dominican Republic."

In talking with Samantha and Matt, I discovered what I suspect doctors all know, and that is that kids today have a much different relationship to diabetes than I did—and do. To me it was an occasion to feel frustration and fear and discomfort. After some fifty thousand injections, I am no longer self-conscious about having to test or inject in public given no other choice, but in the early days, I would search down a ladies' room no matter how hard it was to find. On one such occasion, after giving myself an injection, I wrongly threw the empty, capped syringe into the wastebasket by the sink while I washed my hands. A few minutes later, a woman came out of her stall and noticed the syringe. She clucked her tongue, shook her head, and said to me, "These drug addicts. They're everywhere!"

I felt hounded, resentful, embarrassed, and generally ticked off at the difficulties of juggling everything successfully and still maintaining a shred of self-esteem—even if she didn't know the syringe was mine.

But today the technology is so advanced, glucose monitors are so sophisticated, software interfaces so intricate, needles so thin, insulin so adjustable, pumps so much like PDAs and video games that the youngsters are adept at using, that kids feel they have a much better chance of escaping complications, and much to appreciate about how diabetes has shaped their lives. They are counseled by diabetes educators, advised by nutritionists, coached by athletes who know firsthand exactly what to do to make it possible to be an athlete and have diabetes.

These young people are inspiring to me, just as the researchers expanding the frontiers of our knowledge about diabetes are inspiring. For as resilient and determined as diabetes has proven to be, people with the disease are even more resilient and more determined. We at JDRF—and the hundreds of thousands of young people who inspire us every day—know that science will meet the challenges head-on with an arsenal of information. The cure will come.

3

A Walk on the Avenue

Spontaneity is one of the first of life's pleasures that's lost when diabetes appears. Everything must be thought out carefully before doing almost anything. No one likes to give up any sort of freedom, but when dealing with diabetes, there are some things one must accept. This and other matters fall under the heading of control. If you don't control diabetes, it will control you.

Let me tell you what I know (not necessarily what I do—we can aspire together). When you have diabetes, you are responsible for making sure that you are moderate in all things—and if moderation is not really your natural state, well, then try being fanatically moderate, because the middle ground is your Garden of Eden. Your blood sugar can't be too high or too low. Your weight needs to be trim, not heavy, but too thin makes it tough to get a handle on your blood sugar. Stress? A little intensity keeps you alert and vigilant. Too much sends glucose levels soaring and adds to cardiovascular complications. You need enough sleep, but not too much; some carbs, not too many. You get the picture.

For me, the whole process of asserting control has come

into sharper focus in recent years since I have started seeing Carol Levy, M.D., a physician at Weill Cornell Medical College with board certifications in diabetes, endocrinology, and metabolism, just in the last couple of years. She was recommended by a physician friend of mine (also a diabetic) who told me about her new diabetologist (again, a diabetic herself) who put her on an insulin pump and educated her about its use through the aid of a team consisting of the doctor, a diabetes educator, and a nutritionist.

I made an appointment with Dr. Levy and knew immediately that her personality and way of thinking were what I needed. In her small, paper-stacked office, she looks more like the mom of three young children, which she is, than the world-respected diabetes clinician and researcher that she also is. Her long brown hair frames an open face, often crossed by a smile that seems to say, "Isn't this a great challenge we share?"

I have the wonderful feeling that this down-to-earth woman also has common sense and, oh, of course, is a genius. I sense she will help me become the person my fellow diabetics assume me to be.

Since that first meeting, she has helped me see that at some time or another, everyone gets angry and frustrated about having diabetes. This is particularly true when your blood sugar is out of whack and you don't know why. It happens to me sometimes when my diet is pretty stable, exercise is pretty consistent, I'm not fighting a cold or the flu, and yet the fasting readout can be more than 250. And my bedtime reading often is too low for comfort, so I drink some orange juice or cherry juice to cover sleep without having to greet a low at three or four A.M.

I'm also factoring in the amount of Lantus (a long-acting insulin that establishes a steady baseline to cover me during the night hours) I take, which is new to me. Dr. Levy and I are due for another chat. Fast-forward: So I ask her, "What's going on with my blood sugar and what are you going to do about it?"

Calmly she explains, "Ten to fifteen percent of the time, we just don't know what's gone wrong. Perhaps you injected into a bad spot, or you ate some mystery food or were under stress. Sometimes it is a matter of not having enough data. It's hard to keep records, so we can't figure out why blood sugar levels are all over the place. But sometimes, if you really tease it out, you find out the person ate a lot more carbohydrates than she thought, or we didn't realize how a certain kind of exercise—and you do a lot of exercise—was going to affect someone."

So together we began this brand-new (to me) process of figuring out exactly how I could establish better control. She gave me a chart to fill out with what I ate each day, and what my glucose levels were before and after eating, so I could learn how the food I took in was affecting my blood sugar. I also kept tabs on my carbohydrate intake and my insulin—both basal and fast-acting. I entered exercise information, too, and an occasional test for ketones.

Tracking your every move is a lot of work—or so it seems to me—and it occupies a lot of thought and time until it becomes a habit. Then you can do it without it interfering with day-to-day living. One of the things that Dr. Levy has taught me is the very latter-day revelation of how to select the right amount of an insulin bolus.

I'd not even been familiar with the word. It's an amount of insulin to be taken to cover carbohydrates in food. It hadn't occurred to me that there existed blocks of time in a given day when a blood sugar test was in order for me. So I rarely looked. But if I had and it was high—What to do? What to do? If I did nothing, then the next premeal test would be through the cathedral ceiling! All in all, the new routine has worked out well for me, and my A1C's are much better.

Of course, you'll have to work out a schedule with your doctor. Or (hopefully) you're already on top of it. The lesson here is: *Continue to ask questions!* It's never too late.

We are lucky that diabetes is a disease over which we have some power. There is always hope and always something that can make our lifestyle better. Sometimes you can achieve that through a nice, orderly, step-by-step process. And sometimes you have to learn how to do that through trial and error. That was certainly true for me in the years immediately following my diagnosis.

I'll never forget one warm and sticky New York day. I was strolling up Madison Avenue in a "honeymoon state"—that is, as of yet no diabetic consequence had befallen me. My glucose levels had been quite reasonable; I had the timing of self-administered tests and insulin injections under control, after only a matter of weeks—"What a champ you are, kid!"

I was enjoying myself, window-shopping, and even though the weather was warm, I was surprised when my reflection in a storefront revealed dark stains on my favorite shirt. Hmmm, I was perspiring like a racehorse. No, like a farm animal. Suddenly I felt like I was sinking into a swamp of anxiety.

I passed a DIG WE MUST sign with all the attendant cacophony: the drilling, rhythmic hammering, and, of course, New York drivers' answers to anything daring to interrupt their otherwise "peaceful" flow of traffic—a barrage of a thousand car horns, screeching musical invectives. It all added to my feeling of panic.

I was surprised to find myself digging around in my handbag. For what? I couldn't remember. Ah yes, Life Savers! I had been told to keep Life Savers always with me in case I experienced an episode of low blood sugar. I preferred all cherry. Yes! That's what it was, low blood sugar! I was now trying to deal with the shakes as I continued my own digging when— eureka!—under a crumpled handkerchief and just to the right of my wallet there lurked my salvation. Have you ever tried to open a roll of Life Savers when your hands are shaking? It ranks up there with opening the packaging of a CD.

Remembering a coffee shop up ahead, I popped red Life Savers as I trundled my way in what I hoped was the right direction. I worried terribly about how it was going to look—my bursting in, asking for a glass of orange juice: "What's the matter with that woman?" "Is that Mary Tyler Moore?" "She's all rumpled and sweaty. She was never like that with Dick Van Dyke." I bellied up to the bar and ordered a large orange juice. No one even looked at me. Ten minutes later, all was well. But I did pop into the drugstore to buy a carton of red Life Savers.

Little did I know that the dips and blips of hypoglycemia would plague me for years to come. The lowest I've gone is 24, an event I hope never to repeat. But there is a bit of good news for all of us who have suffered repeated episodes—recent research has suggested that, for most people, hypoglycemia causes no deleterious effects on the brain, it just feels that way

while you are in the middle of the muddle. I've been so mud-
dled on occasion that the fact of my diabetes doesn't register
and I become convinced that I'm simply losing my mind—a
mean-spirited and dangerous trick that diabetes pulls on you.
Until a relatively short time ago (the mid-1930s, I think), people
with type 1 diabetes who displayed strange behavior in public
as a result of extreme low blood sugar were considered to be
bizarre personalities. Knowing little about diabetes, well-meaning
policemen would haul off these sufferers to the nearest mental
institution, where they would remain until they were tracked
down by loved ones!

But even today, when the world is a kinder place for those
so afflicted, it's important to keep your senses attuned to your
body's clues to a dropping glycemic level so that it can be
doused with orange juice, glycemic tablets, or Life Savers. Dr.
Levy recommends glucose tablets. Although I have never been
a fan—favoring something with a more rewarding flavor—her
reasons are sound: "I think glucose tablets are the best for several reasons," she says. "They do work the quickest and there is
less temptation to overeat them since they really don't taste
that good. And they are easy to carry and have a long life.

"I have no objection to people using Life Savers or the
four-ounce juice boxes. The recommendation is about fifteen
grams of carbohydrate, which is the four-ounce juice box, about
six Life Savers, or about three glucose tablets. When you are
low it is hard to chew a bunch of Life Savers, and they don't
work as quickly . . . like your story on Madison Avenue, Mary,
where you were trying to find the Life Savers. For people who
don't like the glucose tablets, the four-ounce juice box really

can work—just throw it in your purse. Sometimes it is hard to chew when you are really low."

A caution here: Whatever your choice of lifesaving magic, the need to put it into your system is so great that one tends to overdo it and ends up sending blood sugar readings sky-high. Once you have taken your emergency glucose booster, wait fifteen minutes, check your sugar to see where you are, and adjust accordingly. I hear Dr. Levy's advice every time: "It can be scary, but try to let yourself sit there and wait. If you feel like you need to put something in your mouth, choose something like a piece of cheese, which won't raise your blood sugar. Then if in fifteen minutes you still feel shaky, you may need to eat something else. When you feel really terrible, it's hard to wait, but it is important to do so. And it's also important to realize that low blood sugar can produce a false sense of hunger—it will go away as your glucose levels rises—but you must wait."

Still, after almost forty years of counting and calculating with some success, I notice that the severity of my low readings is worsening and that these episodes come on with less warning.

Many things in life seem to come without warning, even if they might be predicted by some objective scientist studying the way our day-to-day lives unfold. So in 1980, feeling a bit wobbly and light-headed, unsure of how to take the next step, I parted from Grant. Having made it through nearly eighteen years as a couple blessed with love and success, we began, each of us, to count (separately, of course) the number of meaningless arguments that were becoming a dark presence in our lives, something almost tangible. Or did I create that cloud in my own mind?

Drinking, though carefully kept under wraps, was altering us, inside and out. And a bitterness developed that nearly broke our hearts.

Grant once said, "I never heard Mary complain about the diabetes during our marriage." He meant that as praise for my ability to be strong, but I think now that that statement is evidence of what was wrong with us. We never shared our fears or showed any kind of weakness. And the fear of revealing too much was always there. Nonetheless, I don't think the dissolution of marriage counted as a complication of diabetes.

4

Testing, Testing

Seven years after *The Mary Tyler Moore Show* became such a hit with the critics and viewers, our writers/producers decided to look for new challenges, something we actors knew was probably best for us all to be thinking about as well. But it would have been blasphemous to let that suspicion take form in words. We didn't talk about our futures; the present was too rapturous. This show was what we did, it was who we were. Leave? Stop? No! Impossible!

Our merry band kept playing until Grant told me the writers' decision was a fait accompli. They were leaving and so was the show. Without the guidance and input of its creators, the show, even with new and talented writers, would never be the same.

And so, like children packing up their things before moving on to college, remembering the Christmas that occasioned a favorite toy, the time that went into the watercolor living on the back of the bathroom door, pretty much always covered by a bathrobe, we who would soon depart would take note of the familiar items, like the hide-a-bed couch in the living room set where we'd gather for notes after dress rehearsal, each rushing for a more comfortable seat than that couch would provide.

That letter "M" that hung on a wall of the living room set was a prize that everyone begged to have as a memento, but their requests were denied. It would live in their memories, but would reside in my house.

The "M" belongs to me! And, as I am, 'tis a hearty old thing. It was sent to L.A. in 1991 for the taping of a retrospective of the show and, after its three-thousand-mile trip, was accidentally dropped and shattered into several pieces. It's fine now—you can't even see a scar after those collagen injections!

So it was that 1980 saw a newly single, terrified "forty-two-year-old virgin" begin a "never-before-attempted!" (in her life, anyway) feat: living an independent life. I wouldn't have thought of doing this without a prompt, but I was asked to star in the play *Whose Life Is It Anyway?* on Broadway, and that served as the setting for my big growth spurt. It was an invitation I couldn't refuse. So I packed up my syringes, test strips, and some New York–ish clothes and moved to Manhattan to prove I could bring something to the role of a quadriplegic young man who fights for the right to die. Yes, I said man! The play tells of a young, vital sculptor who loses the use of his arms and legs in an auto accident and who, after reviewing the absence of purpose and pleasure in his new life, initiates a fight for the right to end it.

The role of the patient was initially played, and beautifully so, by Tom Conti, who, after a six-month run, longed to be with his family in Scotland.

The play's producer, Emanuel Azenberg, a great creative

force and now a dear friend, called my agent, John Gaines, about the interest in and availability of Richard Thomas to take over for Tom. Well, alas, "Mr. Thomas is unavailable," he said, "but what about Mary Tyler Moore?" (Just that quickly!)

"No, no, no," Manny Azenberg replied. "It's a male role."

"Nonsense!" my very creative and determined agent responded. "It's a nightmare situation that could befall anyone. It's an asexual role requiring only a good performer."

"Let me ask the playwright, Brian Clark, how he feels about it," said Manny, warming to the idea. "At the very least it requires the changing of a lot of pronouns and a few casting changes. But this could be a never-before-done milestone. And I'd love to give the play another few more months after Tom leaves."

The prospect of doing the part was exhilarating and a bit frightening. It was the first time that I was to be on my own! Everything in the world around me seemed unfamiliar, new and unnerving, but struggle through the unfamiliar I definitely had to do. I did my best to focus on the independent, new girl in town that Mary Richards was to Minneapolis, but I had taken on the challenge of New York City! A little applause here, please!

With Richie ensconced in his own apartment while finishing up high school and working part-time as an assistant to the head still photographer at CBS Television, I followed my instincts and shuffled off to Buffalo. Well, to New York City.

My first executive decision was to move into an apartment-like suite in the Waldorf Towers on Park Avenue. From my perspective today I can see how cosseted I was there, where I became a modern-day version of Eloise at the Plaza, sur-

rounded by people who were paid to be caring parents. I had
an apartment with a full, if tiny, kitchen. Even if I didn't use it,
the presence of cooking machines and utensils allowed me to
call my new dwelling a home. Mostly, room service saw to my
every gustatory whim: one six-minute egg, dark toast, please,
and juice with my coffee. One day I'd learn to prepare it all by
myself.

Alas, growing up the only daughter of a reluctant cook, I
had to rely instead on the kindness of strangers—room service, of course, the friendly concierge who welcomed my safe
return at day's end, and the hotel's florist, who daily saw to
a single rose for my desk. It was, ironically, a constant re-
minder of the self-reliant actress I seemed to be while doing
The Mary Tyler Moore Show—analyzing scenes, making decisions on how to interplay a scene with Ed or Valerie, memoriz-
ing the dialogue. (I was the only cast member who was absent
from the gag reel each year, because I never made mistakes!)
I never let anyone treat me like the boss, and yet, that's what
I was. So on the one hand I excelled as a professional, and on
the other, I feared that I was failing miserably on a personal
level.

Do I remember how my diabetes was doing? In truth, not
really. I tried to make it the last thing on my mind, without
neglecting the basics. I kept my insulin in the little fridge at
the Waldorf, my syringes tucked into a dresser drawer. I was
deep into rehearsals and then the performances of the play.
That took almost every waking hour. When I went out on
dates, I didn't mention it if they didn't already know about
the diabetes. How did I feel? I guess I was tired sometimes.
Shaky. Grumpy. Back then there weren't A1C tests, so I have

no idea how my blood sugars measured up over time. But I don't remember any major highs or lows that knocked me out of commission. I was intently focused on getting through each day in my brave new world. And get through I did. Somehow I had a great time. The play got really good reviews and I was honored with a Tony Award for my performance.

It was tougher when the agreed-to four-month run of the play came to an end and I was forced to explore New York City and my new life. Then I got scared. And I was pretty hard on myself—thinking that I was a real failure at this grown-up role.

Since then, one of the things that has helped me be more generous toward myself—and consequently toward others—is my interaction with young people who have diabetes. They are so outspoken about their fears and worries. I hear my own, often unspoken ones, echoed in their candid conversations. Sometimes it brings me up short, but I appreciate the end results.

Allison Shyer, now seventeen, has been contending with diabetes for twelve years, so there's very little she hasn't seen or thought about when it comes to coping with the disease. I asked her to come to talk with me and some other young people about her experiences and feelings. "I know college is coming, but right now I would be scared to live on my own," she told me. "Last summer when I was at sleepaway camp I managed my diabetes better than I thought I would. I think being away from home made me more diligent about like checking my blood sugar, 'cause I knew if I messed up there would be nobody to fix it for me. I had to step up.

"My mom is very aware of how I'm doing. She says she

internalizes my day—what I ate, my schedule. Sometimes she will sit bolt upright in bed at three A.M., grab a meter, and have me test for low blood sugar."

I think I may have wished I had a parent watching over me—out on my own, in New York, in 1980, with diabetes. So what did I do? I came up with a brilliant idea: Take Mom and Dad to Europe! I was obviously so scared that I'd go to any lengths to avoid my self-imposed "solo" trial. Little did I realize that this trip would involve two pretty amazing men and add fresh impetus to my growing up again.

Having flown on the Concorde several times, I crowned myself Chief Educator and Calmer of Mom and Dad, reminding them that Mach 2 smashes the sound barrier, not to worry if, at that point, you feel a speeding up of the plane, and that the toilets on the Concorde make a sudden and horrendous noise when flushed. "Not to worry. Nothing is wrong with the plane"—a parent calming her children in reverse.

My dad, who so enthusiastically read me every one of the Oz books, was bereft of the ability to express his love for me—or anyone. But he was startlingly handsome as well as glib, witty, cutting. Sometimes I long to sit at David Letterman's knee and have him read me stories.

My mother was an entertaining alcoholic, who would drink very heavily for a week or two and then sober up at my dad's "final" demand. When I was in grammar school, on the walk home I would be unsure of what to expect. Who would open the door? The good mom or the unknowable creature that drink produced?

Taking them on this trip was an opportunity for us to get to know one another better. One thing they didn't get to know or understand any better was my daily struggle with diabetes. I don't think Mom or Dad ever wrestled with the Genealogical Blame Game—Dad's research into his family history hadn't turned up any diabetes in previous generations, and Mom just didn't know one way or the other. They were, in fact, pretty relaxed about it all. I didn't test in front of them or take injections while we were together (in those days, I was still scurrying to the bathroom to give myself a shot). Their apparent indifference was reassuring in a way. No big deal. There may have been more percolating under the surface. I do remember an occasion when my mother, having just baked a pineapple upside-down cake (my absolute favorite of all time), offered me a slice, and then withdrew it, saying, "Oh, that's right. You don't like cake anymore. Won't you change your mind?"

My mother's inability to understand the seriousness of diabetes sometimes seemed like a refusal to know me. When one's mother is an alcoholic and, despite a child's pleading with her to stop, she continues, you may read that as a cold, selfish act on her part. It hurts, but most people can't stop drinking at will. I didn't know that then, nor did she, and I'm sure it broke her heart as she discovered she couldn't do it alone. It takes deep self-analysis with ongoing guidance from a counselor, and for most (including me), involvement in a 12-step program.

Seven years before my mother's death from a brain hemorrhage, my brother, John, and I staged an intervention, along with several family members and friends. During a two-hour session of open-ended discussions, we were able to convince her to seek help at the Betty Ford Center, where I had been treated a few years previously. It worked! It was not easy for her, but she stuck with it, going to meetings every day for the first year of her sobriety, and, my oh my, she took it very seriously.

John and I had our mother back (did we ever really have her to begin with?), and it was a gift from heaven getting to know this new person who seemed to love us more with the passing days.

Anyway, as we headed out on our joint adventure, with my hopes that it would bring us closer, you can see that I had a major task in front of me. The trip did let me find out how organized I could be, planning the itinerary, booking hotels, hiring the drivers for trips through England, France, and Italy. And all followed by *a private audience with Pope John Paul II* arranged through the kindness of Monsignor William O'Brien of New York City, the guiding light of Daytop Village, the famed drug rehabilitation center for young people worldwide. This is the pinnacle of any Catholic's life (even a twice-divorced one as I am). My father was a lifelong devout Catholic and my mother a recent convert to Catholicism. This was going to be a truly important experience for them and for their wayward daughter.

From early in his papacy this pope seemed to embody life's zest—its music and dance, all the arts. No doubt this was spurred by his youthful involvement in writing plays and poetry. And let's not forget that he had been an actor, as well.

At the same time, it turns out he was a man of little fondness for pomp and circumstance. In fact, about two weeks before our departure came word from the pope's chief of protocol stating that the Holy Father's wishes were that we forgo the centuries-old custom of kissing his ring—"a simple handshake would suffice." And the ladies were not required to wear the black long-sleeved frocks and black lace head coverings that were traditional. He wanted his audiences to feel comfortable with him—all under God, not as humbled subjects.

I admired his concept, but I confess my disappointment over the new nondress code. Much as I would help choose the best costume for a role, I'd spent a good deal of time trying to put together a flawless approximation of what I'd been told was the traditional garb. Why did he have to do away with this particular pomp?

An awareness of fashion, color, style, and fun was something I had at an early age. I think I must have been three or four when, on Christmas Day, I adorned myself with all the crumpled, discarded ribbons from the packages by tying them around my head. You can just imagine the self-appointed queen, crowned with tangled tendrils of ribbons nearly masking her happy face. I still do a less exotic, conservative version from time to time at birthday parties and such—even without a drink. Well, it makes the cleanup a little easier for the hostess.

On the appointed day, the pope's nearly apoplectic visitors—about a dozen of us, Catholics, Jews, and Protestants, all devoted to Monsignor O'Brien and his works—were taken by van to beautiful Castel Gandolfo, a small castle nearly hidden in the hilly terrain about eighteen miles southeast of the Vatican. It served as a country estate where the pomp was held to a minimum and circumstances were not so overwhelming.

It was here that the pope would receive us and say Mass in

his private chapel, which looks to be a miniature version of the Sistine Chapel. It has historic carvings, frescoes, beautiful murals, and the aura of an ancient symphony being played yet barely heard. I swear there was a light mist surrounding us.

As we awaited his appearance in the reception room, we exchanged nervous chatter, one or two of the ladies expressing the need for a powder room, "or was there enough time? Would there even be such a thing in here?"

Suddenly, he appeared in the doorway, several black-clad aides accompanying him and, just as suddenly, the room went silent with awe and nervousness. The new knowledge of his warmth and humanity and the absence of ring kissing caused me (I can't be sure of the others) to be unsure of what constituted appropriate behavior and respect. How does one act without the ring kissing? "Hello. I've heard so much about you"?

With his arms outstretched in welcome, he moved to every person, saying a few words to each. When he came toward me smiling, as he had for the others, I found myself in a half curtsy, knee bent in supplication, trying desperately not to lose my balance. This is where his welcoming outstretched arms did much more than greet me. They saved me.

I can't bring back the words he spoke, but I will never forget his piercing blue eyes as they peered—no, knifed—their way into mine. I was riveted, unable to function, form words, or look away. I didn't want to, anyway. He owned me for those few seconds and there was only one message: He approved! It was to make a change in me. If he thought I was a worthy person, this pope, this man, a reigning king, why didn't I? Couldn't I look for the strength that he obviously saw in me? Couldn't I build on this enormous experience?

I've only been so affected by one other person, and that was Frank Sinatra—just one moment, an introduction, eye contact. But there was no further growth on my part from that experience.

The pope excused himself to change into the vestments for saying Mass and we were escorted into the chapel, where he would soon join us.

The issue of Communion came thundering into my head. I was no longer a practicing Catholic, having, in timid steps, departed from the Church's dogma years before. Then too, I was married and divorced for the second time and was no longer in a "state of grace." Doctrine forbids a second marriage after the dissolution of a valid first one. I kept thinking, "I am a good person. The pope thinks I'm a good person." But still, I wasn't worthy of inclusion in this rite.

The Holy Father entered the chapel and knelt before the small but ornate altar. His face was intense with concentration and worry. He knelt, rested his elbows on the marble railing in front of him, clasped his hands in prayer, and pressed his forehead to them.

At the point in the Mass when the priest (this was no priest—it was the pope!) blesses the wafer and beckons for the pure to step forward, I had to resist the urge to shout, "I'm coming! Please, wait for me." A drum was beating staccato rhythms at the back of my head. I tried to decipher the feelings that drum brought forth in me. It was pride. This was my house for many years. Longing, too. It might win my father's favor. I was making a decision. I felt a curiously guiltless right to receive Communion again, in this moment, from this pope, who would surely understand and forgive me for breaking the law, and through him I would have God's understanding. And the decision was made. But the knowledge of how to stand, turn in place, and then walk had escaped me. I crouched like a frightened squirrel, but then the sense memory of ambulatory basics returned and I somehow stood and made my way to the altar. Watching me must have made my father so proud, especially if I weren't struck dead in the process. And with each footfall I expected that a shaft of piercing light, or something, would thrust itself through the dome above to smite me (right in the heart) and prevent my impending sacrilege. But it didn't. And there I was on my knees at the altar railing and Pope John Paul II was smiling down at me. I received the Host, bent my head, and thanked God for this saint of a man.

Returning to the pew, I knelt and from my (still intact) peripheral vision I could see my parents smile at me. And with the Host still in my mouth, I did my best to smile back. They looked at me from time to time, but they never asked me if I planned to return to the Church. As we knelt in our pew, my father put his hand over mine and patted it, whispering, "Well done, chum."

To this day, I don't know his intention behind that uplifting little tribute. Did he think I'd be returning to the Catholic Church? Or was it a salute to my throwing away the monstrous fear of dogma and allowing the moment to happen (something he could never do)? In not knowing, I came to embrace him (well, sling an arm around his shoulders with compassion). Yet, still, I was unable to express it. I could see this scene on film: a three-shot of our eyes darting one way and the other, never in the same direction at the same time.

In retrospect, the strength I was to develop, the belief in myself, was sparked by that moment.

I have not returned to the Catholic Church formally as yet, but I have a sense of God in my life now. He walked right in when I opened the door with Pope John Paul II's hand on mine.

5

Step-by-Step

I returned to my still-unconquered city, an exhausted Mom and Dad in tow. They were to stay with me for a few days of further "tripping the light fantastic"—theater, Statue of Liberty, and such. But my mother was suffering symptoms of a bronchial infection, which had begun in Paris, and wasn't she proud of that—"Yeah, I picked up the bug in Paris." She was also smoking nearly two packs a day (almost up to my level of three), and dealing with her promised abstinence from alcohol—no small amount of stress there. So I called my internist, but it was Yom Kippur and he was at temple. I was, however, given the name and number of Dr. S. Robert Levine, who was completing his fellowship (specialty training in cardiology) at Mount Sinai Medical Center.

Reaching Dr. Levine by phone, I gave him my mother's history, which included a small stroke suffered only a few months before.

"Can you bring her to the hospital?"

If she'll agree to go, I told him.

"Let me speak to her," he said matter-of-factly.

My mother? My mother going to a hospital? I don't think

so. She was a very witty, sometimes even outspoken person who could talk her way in to or out of almost anything. But while she was on the phone I heard her laugh and say, "Yes, yes, you're so kind. I see. Thank you. We'll be right there, Doctor." I couldn't wait to meet this miracle man!

The ride in the cab was as serious as it would be in a film about someone facing death. No talk, only grimly staring straight ahead, her coughs interrupting the silence from time to time.

Entering the emergency room, which was remarkably calm, I jumped as a nurse approached from nowhere to say, "The doctor will see you now." I wondered how many times I'd said those very words in an episode of one or more medical series that blanketed the airwaves. And I thought, I hope I said the line better than she did.

That's when the nurse indicated a tall, dark, and yes, handsome man in a doctor's white coat leaning against an open doorjamb, one foot casually crossed over the other as he intently looked over some information on a clipboard. As we neared him, he looked up, smiled briefly, and extended his hand. "I'm Dr. Levine." There was not the slightest glimmer of recognition of who I might be, beyond the nervous daughter of an ailing, difficult mother. After introductions and a few pleasantries, I watched my mother interact with him. Even though he was a bit overwhelmed by her talkative nature, I saw a firm but gentle man take her elbow and, smiling reassurance to me, lead her to an exam room. I was at peace.

Dad and I passed the time making stilted conversation in the waiting room during which he upped his volume and proclaimed, "I don't like this pope, never have." A smile acknowledging the irony of it all crossed his face, or was it his enjoyment of bursting my bubble?

I'd convinced myself that an audience with the leader of the Catholic Church—the pope!—would surely bring my father to his knees in awe and coax from him a smile for his daughter. But there wasn't even a "Sorry you went to the trouble, chum." Just, "I prefer that all popes be of Roman descent."

Interrupting this blow, Mom and Dr. Levine emerged from the exam room laughing like old friends.

"I think these antibiotics will do," he said. "And I'd like to see her at home tomorrow since she must fly the following day. Tomorrow is my day off, but I'd like to have another listen."

"No, we can't do that to you, Doctor. It isn't fair," I replied. And then I thought of my mother, how frail she was, and how attractive he was, and I handed him my address. Mary, what were you thinking!?

I think a could-be romance with him was brewing even then. There was, of course, the man/woman tension and, after a conversation the next day at my apartment, the discovery of our shared interests—love of animals, theater, art, and, oh yes, Mom's temperature was back to normal, politics (at a safe distance), plus a preference for slow tempos. But accelerating my curiosity about him was a review of my past choices in men: I'd allowed myself to be taken care of twice by older men who, like my father, expected a kind of obeisance. The power positions they held in my mind (if not in the world) made it easier for me to be the best good girl I could be instead of being a partner. During my marriage to Grant, why, for God's sake, did I never take advantage of the infrastructure that was MTM Enterprises and develop a movie for TV or a film for myself when the MTM show came to an end? Why did I choose to wait for the phone to ring?

I can't lay all the responsibility for my stunted growth on others, because I knew what was happening and willingly allowed it, enjoying, for a time, my role as princess in training. There it is again—I didn't plan to say those words. They just presented themselves to prove my point.

With Robert it promised to be different. In this relationship, I sensed, I might be able to take the initiative in my own life now and then, actually choosing where we'd live, what car I'd drive. This may have been the ironic result of Robert's view (or lack of view) of me. One of the most interesting aspects of our first encounters (at least to me) was that the man had been involved in medical studies during the seventies and just didn't have the time to watch television. I don't think he had ever seen my show and he barely knew who I was. He was probably learning how to read during *Van Dyke*!

There was quite an age difference between us then, almost eighteen years, but not now. It doesn't exist. Being married twenty-five years has a way of bridging real and imagined gaps. We've had a few arguments, forgivenesses, solid discussions of politics, family matters that have been equitably solved with his help. He would expect me to add that last part. And it's true. He stands beside me always, sometimes badgering me into taking better care of myself, making me mad—and making me laugh. And laugh we do (after some sulking and mental replays of what we said, which then, of course, can lead to round two).

Part of the challenge was and is that he is an alpha dog, and I was gleefully developing my own alpha instincts. We each found it blindingly difficult to relent, even when I was the correct dog and each of us knew it. In fact, some of the most gorgeous fights I've had with my husband have centered on the management of my diabetes. Robert is a cardiologist with infinite knowledge of the digestive and vascular aspects of diabetes. But I've owned the disease for more than half my life and think I've earned the right to make my own mistakes and decisions about how to handle it. As a result of our vigorous discussions, my husband and would-be endocrinologist carries many psychological black-and-blue marks. He could tell you about a very different Mary from the one that the public usually hears about, because even though I'm a grown-up (or at least, growing up!), there still exists within me that child I thought I'd left behind in Brooklyn, where I was born. She visits from time to time, and when she does she riles me up, and I start slinging arrows and stones at those nearest and dearest to me.

Now wouldn't you think they'd keep those weapons out of a child's grasp? But love Robert I do and he me.

Together we have faced many of the tough times that families encounter; loss and renewal come in waves. And underneath and around it all has been the constant of diabetes and its slowly encroaching complications that alter my every day in ways subtle and profound.

6

Foot First

One of the big challenges that Robert and I faced together happened in 1995 when I returned to network television with a stab at a new series, *New York News*. In the hour-long drama with a splash of humor, I played the managing editor of a daily New York tabloid newspaper. Make that the tough managing editor. (Think Lou Grant in drag.)

I thought broad-shouldered suits and high, pointy-toed, spiky shoes would take some of the responsibility for the characterization off my shoulders. It was the feet that did me in. Well, an appendage of same. A terrible blister arose on my left small toe and it wasn't responding to treatment. (The show itself was one big blister, in fact, soon to be lanced.) I was on my feet for ten or eleven hours a day, so wearing those all-important pointy shoes contributed to my now-frightening toe situation. We had one day of filming left to do, and as soon as I was finished, my toe and I were taken to the hospital, where I would pay for my "actress indulgence shoes."

At the hospital the next morning I thanked everybody for their care and told them that I had two dogs at home longing for their mother, and so would they please unhook the IV and let me go there. "No." They would not indulge that maternal request.

When Robert came in, a nurse took him aside and apparently told him about my pathetic request to leave. In less than a second he knifed himself across the room to my bedside and initiated a grip on my hand that with any further pressure could have qualified me for hospitalization on its own. This is something that happens when he's administering psychological help, too. He is so concerned with helping me when my sugar is very low that it turns into what appears to be anger, which causes me to appear to be frightened, as well as depressed.

"Do you want to undergo the salami process? Because you still have an infection there and if they have to remove that toe, which very well may happen, in time the infection can spread, and before long they'll remove the ball of your foot as well, then later move a bit north, taking off the rest of your foot. It's a slice-by-slice procedure done over time. You will stay here with the IV in place until your toe is perfectly clean."

My husband and his colleagues often alleviated the pressures of completing their fellowships in cardiology by taking up the lingo of their predecessors, using humorous (at least they thought so) insider jargon regarding new patients and such. If a drug addict arrives with no symptoms demanding a workup, for example, he's called a "Gomer" (Get Out of My Emergency Room!). The occasional newborn of an alcoholic mother sometimes shows the effects with uneven or off-center features. The infant is referred to as an "F.L.K." (Funny-Looking Kid). This last abbreviation, I'm told, is used in many hospitals. I, too, exhibit off-center and uneven features, not grossly evident, but enough to qualify me as the F.L.K. daughter of an alcoholic mother. Nobody really understood the sensitivity of the fetus so long ago.

On day three, I sat in my bed, foot hoisted above my heart, in the middle of a beautifully appointed enormous room, indulging in enormous self-pity.

I felt no pain, as the foot was desensitized due to diabetic neuropathy, anyway. So I had plenty of time to focus on the very real threat of amputation. I'd been doing an excellent job of imagining the horrors of missing a small toe with partial removal of the platform supporting it, giving no small amount of morbid conjecture to the subsequent salami process that would surely follow. It was Robert who interrupted my "worst-case scenario" with his third floral offering in as many days. It was so good to have him there with his reassurances and treasured sarcasm—"You're pretty well set up here, aren't you?"

"But why can't I be home in my smaller bedroom with 'the kids'?" I whined.

"Hey, blockhead," he said with a smile, "you're on the road home already. Be patient." And as he offered that exquisite advice, a thought, or rather a "Lucy"-like plot began to take shape.

In chatting with the head of patient relations, a very kind woman who visited from time to time, a woman who earlier professed great love of the Van Dyke show and mine, I learned she was one of the first in her position to avail herself of the Delta Society's patient program using animal therapy. But, knowing about the red tape that would likely be required to bring animals into the hospital, even under the society's auspices, I thought it would be wise to ask her about the possibility of allowing my two dogs (a golden retriever named Dash and a Petit Basset Griffon Vendéen hound named Dudley) to come pay me a psychologically necessary clandestine visit.

After her face returned to its normal musculature, she smiled and said, "There's no way we could bring the dogs in here through a normal process. But," she added, "it's pretty quiet in this wing right now. Maybe we could sneak them in for a visit." And then she giggled and said, "Oh, wouldn't that be fun. Let me think about it." As she was leaving, she turned and asked, "Do they bark?"

Never, I lied.

"Good," she responded.

This angel of mercy returned later to tell me that the head of security thought it would be a great caper and would be happy to help in any way that he could. My friend and assistant, Terry, brought the four-legged contraband to the hospital in a limo with blacked-out windows and was met on the sidewalk by the security chief, who was pushing a large wheeled plastic hamper pilfered from the laundry into which the "goods" were placed, each doing that nervous tap dance dogs do when they're in unfamiliar circumstances. But they knew Terry quite well and were able to follow his directions. After partially closing the lid, Terry, the chief of security, and the two dogs entered the lobby's elevator bank, where two other members of the security staff held an elevator and prevented others from entering it. The basket, although large, could not altogether contain the golden retriever, whose head kept popping up. But they made it to my floor and entered the room.

I was bursting with joyous anticipation and pride in the

team that had been so successful! When the container had been slowly tipped to its side and opened, two very disoriented dogs stumbled and raced out, putting the lie to my description of how well mannered they would be.

They paid little, if any, attention to me, instead checking out every chair and legs of same, people and their legs, paws up on the windowsills, searching for a notion of where they were. And then they took in my elevated foot and all hell broke loose— many people scrambling to calm and reassure them.

Someone had been thoughtful enough to place a kidney bowl full of water in an out-of-the-way place. The kids were contentedly "schlurping" away when our secret rendezvous was interrupted by a knock on the door. Who could it be? Where can we hide the dogs? How much trouble am I in?

It was my husband, Robert. And his face betrayed shock as he acknowledged the now leaping and barking dogs, who'd managed to step right into the bowl of remaining water, tipping it onto his shoe. You saw that one coming, didn't you?

Thank God for his "ever at the ready" sense of humor. He hugged the dogs and then looked straight at me, wearing one of his most serious faces, and said, "Lucy, you've got a lot of 'splainin' to do."

By the way, he'd stopped in to tell me that I'd be sent home in a few days! Timing, timing, timing!

Timing is everything, don't you think? Maybe not everything, as in "It would have happened to you anyway," but what I'm about to tell you will make you a believer.

Two days later the toe was improving. I was going all weird from boredom and just a touch of self-pity when my agent called to tell me that the film I'd just finished shooting, *Flirting with Disaster,* needed an additional scene for the ending. It was to be shot in one day and it had to be tomorrow. "Why?" I shrieked.

"Because Alan Alda is off to Paris for a starring role in Woody Allen's new movie musical, *Everyone Says I Love You.* Tomorrow is the only day it can be done."

"But I'm in the hospital with an IV of antibiotics in my arm!" I was sobbing with self-pity. "I can't leave or my toe will be salami!" I did call back later to explain more cogently.

It was my doctor—not my live-in, but my internist, Dr. Stanley Mirsky—who understood my predicament. (I was fortunate to find Dr. Mirsky when I first moved to New York a shaky, newly divorced woman who was not only seeking help with her diabetes but with life. And over the years, he was at my side at the hospital on several occasions, fulfilling his commitment that he—my big brother—would always be there.)

I didn't want to be absent from a single frame in the film. Dr. Mirsky asked how the scene would be staged. I told him we'd all be seated at a dinner table. "Good!" he allowed. "We'll have an IV nurse accompany you to the studio. The leg, of course, has to be elevated. You can hide the foot under the table. The IV can be capped off when you're on camera and re-activated when not. I think you'll do just fine," my physician/director said.

We only needed to do this *Keystone Kops* routine a dozen or so times. It worked perfectly, just like in the movies.

We all gathered to see it at a special screening, excited and expectant. When the movie ended and the lights came back on, amid the applause and laughter there sat five grim actors, who, unlike the rest of the audience, laughing and applauding their approval, just sat there with stunned expressions on our faces. The added scene around the table had been cut! It was deemed superfluous by the producers!

This was a terrific film with Ben Stiller, Téa Leoni, Patricia Arquette, Lily Tomlin, George Segal, the soon-to-depart Alan Alda, and me. It was a very funny movie, boasting some splendid performances to be proud of, and great reviews, too! I'll never forget it. And I'll also never forget the image of myself on the set sitting in a wheelchair with an IV running.

Listen, this is important: People with diabetes must give their feet a daily check. It's something that can be done right after showering. Look between each toe, check the bottom of the foot and the heel, where often new shoes will produce a blister. For a large number of diabetics, neuropathy has reduced the feelings in the lower extremities, allowing a potential infection to begin its journey to a full-blown threat.

Over the years Robert has been there to help me contend with all kinds of difficulties and complications. But when the complications of diabetes strike, it's a singularly alone feeling, as I discovered when I began to have trouble with my eyesight, just twelve years after I was diagnosed.

7

Complications

For many years I've been grappling with how responsible I may or may not be for the development of the diabetic complications that have, indeed, presented themselves over time—deterioration of my vision, peripheral artery disease that makes it hard to walk distances, neuropathy in my legs and feet (a dancer's nightmare), and a failing sense of balance (the headers I have taken!).

As my neurologist (doesn't everyone have one?) said to me recently, "I hope in the book you will let readers know that with diabetes there are tough choices to make. Some people, like you, say 'this or that is too much for me to do without.' So you make a choice knowing there are consequences."

I had to admit to Dr. Schaefer that I'm aware in the moment of saying "No way!" and expletives much stronger. So I want to let you, my reader, know that I have not been perfect, that I have made choices (injecting through my pants, eating chocolate mousse without testing, smoking, drinking) that have negative consequences. I don't want you to think that it's okay, or to lead you astray. I think I've had enough comeuppances that the message is clear: You make your choices; you pay the piper.

This is common sense, but it's also been scientifically confirmed through a variety of studies, most notably the Diabetes Complications and Control Trial (DCCT) of 1993. The DCCT clearly showed that the absence of complications was in direct proportion to consistent blood glucose control. In that trial, half of the participants followed an intensive treatment that included testing blood glucose levels four or more times a day; four daily insulin injections with additional boluses (insulin boosters) when necessary; adjustment of insulin doses according to food intake and exercise; a diet and exercise plan; and monthly visits to a health-care team composed of a physician, nurse educator, dietitian, and when indicated, a behavioral therapist.

The results were extraordinary: Among that group, the risk of developing eye disease was reduced by 76 percent; kidney disease—50 percent; nerve disease—60 percent. They also were less likely to develop high cholesterol, a known cause of heart disease.

You can't ever eliminate the risk of these complications completely because the very fact that one is diabetic means that certain biochemical changes have happened in the body that jeopardize the health of large and small blood vessels, alter cellular chemistry, and trigger inflammation, but you can do an enormous amount to reduce the likelihood that you will suffer vision loss, kidney dysfunction, loss of feeling in hands and feet, and other problems. (For more information see the Appendix, page 174.)

I stopped smoking twenty-one years ago. Oh, to have stopped when I was twenty-one years old or, of course, never to have begun. I was fifteen when I had my first cigarette, convincing myself of how sophisticated I was! I would occasionally watch myself smoke in the mirror, devising new and alluring ways to hold the thing, blow out the smoke with multiple expressions and timing. I could find enough silent communication in that cigarette to fill a one-woman play. Sometimes I'd see my expressionless mother and father staring back at me—or was that a dream?

It's odd that children of parents who unintentionally create painful situations in the home—and here I'm talking about violence, smoking, alcoholism—are so often doomed to repeat it.

My best friends at Immaculate Heart High School and I gathered after school every day at a coffee shop on Hollywood Boulevard (near Vine) for the unvarying Coke, fries, and cigarettes. What a sight we must have been, six girls in navy-and-white Catholic girls' school uniforms, fresh-scrubbed faces, and good manners promising a light-filled, happy future, behaving like tramplets from Hollywoodland High. And didn't we love that! It's not easy being a role model in your teens, or at any point, really.

One day my mother, who was a smoker, too, casually asked if smoking would affect the breathing of a dancer. I responded with the conviction of an M.D.: The body adjusts to impediments. It simply pushes more if there's a challenge to the system, Mother. (How's that for on-the-spot lying?) So many dancers smoke it's not even funny!

"Well," she said, lighting another one and laughing at the irony of it, "as long as you keep it quiet, I won't say anything to your father." Now it had the element of real danger. Yet another factor to make it attractive.

I was to become a nearly three-pack-a-day smoker for much of my adulthood. And I know now that it causes the constriction of blood vessels, including those in the retina, the facilitator of sight. So, with every puff, I was asking for the blood vessels to be deprived of oxygen, thereby contributing to the development of diabetic retinopathy and, potentially, blindness.

Adding to the danger to my eyes and cardiovascular system was alcohol. Even though my blood sugars were erratic, I sure drank consistently every evening at six o'clock . . . for many years! I didn't think anyone ever saw me drunk—or was that an illusion? Inside I was scared. I knew I'd gone over an edge, some edge, and I didn't know what to grab for steadiness. I couldn't, wouldn't stop. Some part of my brain functioned well enough, however, to get me to the Betty Ford Center, where in 1984, over a period of five weeks, I grew up some. The counseling at the center helped me to admit my alcoholism, accept it as a fact, and then deal with it.

My experience there was the struggle I somehow knew it would be. As I drank, I had developed comforting habits that I began to see were traps that turned me into a prisoner of my own illusions. Admitting that they were there, and learning to look at my past, both recent and long term, brought me up short at every turn.

I thought I was a good girl. I'd always prided myself on the honesty that had somehow woven itself into the bones and sinew of who I was. I never stole anything as a kid (not after the first time!), rarely lied (except about homework), and yes, I washed my hands after using the toilet—every time.

I think a lot of this unconscious commitment to honesty was instilled in me by my mother, who, upon finding that her "four-year-old thief of a daughter" had purloined a Tootsie Roll from the corner store, simply turned her child around and marched me right back to the lady behind the counter so I could confess to what I'd done. I'll never forget the terror I felt on the walk to the store. Not knowing the magnitude of my crime, my imagination went berserk. What lay ahead for me? Public spanking? Imprisonment? Group yelling at me, even? As I remember it, the owner was most gracious. She winked at this first-time offender.

But at Betty Ford, I had to give up some of my most dearly held ideas about who I was and begin to see myself in the sometimes harsh light of unvarnished reality. The counseling one receives at most rehabilitation centers is modeled around the tenets and structure of a 12-step program. Group members share glimpses into their lives; it is always astounding how listening to the personal stories of the diverse participants, hearing about their fear, anxiety, sorrow, anger, regret, guilt, longing, and jealousy, you feel as though they are talking right to you, about you, about your self-deceptions, your yearnings, your deepest, darkest fears. One of the things you learn very quickly is that no matter what you have chosen to do in your life, you share mutual qualities and flaws with the rest of humanity. Listening and learning in those powerful group settings, I made a pact with myself to allow the hard edges of life to touch me and to stop reaching for a drink to soften the blows.

As with almost all successful campaigns to reach difficult goals, rehabilitation from alcohol can have a positive outcome if you give 100 percent to peeling away the covering that alcohol provides. Truth will out.

In those groups, there were speakers (all recovering alcoholics) who talked about their experiences, and while there was never a story that failed to teach a valuable lesson, one of them captured me wholly. It was told by the lady herself, Betty Ford, the founder of this particular rehabilitation center. Mrs. Ford related how she had tried unsuccessfully to live with or correct chronic back pain by relying heavily on medication. Like many dancers (she had been a member of the Martha Graham Company), she had to contend with a collection of injuries. Add to that the stress of becoming President Gerald Ford's First Lady, and the combination weighed heavily on her, causing her to occasionally take a glass too many from the trays being passed at the many White House functions. But she recognized that her behavior had to change and joined a recovery program. Despite what she described as pit-of-the-stomach fear, she shattered her protective shield of privacy and bravely took her situation to the public.

After her stay at the Long Beach Naval Medical Center in California, where she had been hospitalized for several weeks of detoxification and therapy, she undertook the responsibility for building a larger recovery center, based upon what she had learned there. It was a hands-on commitment in that she not only painstakingly created the curriculum but also spoke to those of us who were there learning from our pasts for the first time.

Her decision was a lifesaver for me and hundreds of thousands of other women who had so much trouble admitting they were alcoholics. You see, at that time (and less so today) many women felt that being a female alcoholic was a disgrace, the lowest of the low, and that an intelligent, well-read, dignified woman couldn't possibly be a drunk. There was so much about Betty Ford that made me feel I could be her sister (except for the First Lady business). She was, first and foremost, a lady (kind, well-mannered, gracious), anything but the commonly held image of an alcoholic woman.

As she took the floor at the center's microphone, I recalled my experience with her while filming a scene for *The Mary Tyler Moore Show*. It had been a short exchange between us over a pair of reading glasses that the President accidentally left behind at a party hosted by Lou Grant and Mary in a hotel. In the scene, Betty Ford called to see if they had been found.

It was a short scene, but she had trouble remembering the dialogue, even as I helped her out by giving her cues while standing just to the side of the camera. I felt so sad that this lovely, warm lady couldn't master it on her own. But the scene, on film, was delightful, and I was told that she remembered her moment of stardom on our show as having been "so much fun."

Now, here we were in a role reversal—she was extending the helpful hand to me, and while at first I felt like an errant schoolgirl, as I identified with her story and digested her almost brutal honesty, I was able to grow emotionally.

Those five weeks at the center transformed my life—and gave me a chance to start growing up—even at my advanced age at the time of forty-five. And so I was growing up again, again. And just in the nick of time, I might add. The alcohol was making my diabetes control inadequate—hell, out of control is the very definition of an alcoholic, even a buttoned-down, polite, and quiet one as I am.

One is never considered cured, even after many years of

sobriety. But by the end of the five weeks I could refer to myself as a recovering alcoholic.

While I can't claim perfection in controlling my diabetes, I can say I haven't had a drink since September 1984. That was three years after I came eye to eye with vision troubles.

8

Second Sight

Sometime in 1981, I began to see strange, irregularly shaped forms floating in my field of vision. You couldn't tell there was anything wrong by looking at me, but what I saw, over a day or so, were vivid red splotches that morphed into black rivulets turning to gray, resembling the trail of a sidewinder in the sand. What was happening to me? Was I going blind? I was terrified.

Robert discovered that the best eye guy was Lawrence A. Yannuzzi, M.D., a well-known professor of clinical ophthalmology at Columbia University Medical School. He is the chief of retinal services, surgeon director and founder and director of the LuEsther T. Mertz Retinal Research Center at the Manhattan Eye, Ear, and Throat Hospital, and president of the Macula Foundation, Inc. He is also the author of more than 375 clinical articles and several textbooks. And with this track record, he dares to be charming and handsome, too.

At our first appointment he asked me to tell him my diabetic history. After I'd finished the tale, I was moved to the examining chair, where my eyes were flooded with a dilating solution, allowing him to peer into the back of the eye—the retina.

What looked like a giant camera suspended from an arm coming from I don't know where was pushed toward my face. My chin rested on a small cuplike tray during the "peering." It took about ten long minutes, during which time only the occasional grunt from him indicated that he was seeing something of note. Good or bad I couldn't tell. His face was hidden by the science-fiction-like apparatus between us, and I was too intimidated by him to ask. So, typically, I assumed that both eyes would have to be removed.

With an "All right, then," he pushed away the Star Wars viewfinder and indicated that I should return to the seat across from him at his desk. When we were settled, he asked when my last eye examination was. I told him that I couldn't recall any during the fifteen years that followed the diabetes diagnosis. "No one cautioned you about the need for vigilant and frequent updates on your status?" he barked.

No, I stammered, wracking my brain for some recollection. I had a hazy sense that it might have been a part of the initial education I'd received at diagnosis. That was in the late sixties— but not in my memory, I confessed to him. Now, I'm sure that I was told about it those many years ago, but since I saw no change in my vision I conveniently put it on my "things to do list."

"You have diabetic retinopathy," he said, looking right at me, no smile on his face.

Retinopathy? The doctor explained that in my case abnormal blood glucose levels over a number of years were the main cause of the problem, since I am very fit and watch my diet and exercise regularly. The retinopathy itself is caused by microvascular abnormalities. As a result of the damage to the small vessels in the eye, a new young army steps in to replace their fallen forebears—this is called neovascularization. Unfortunately, these valiant vessels don't have the strength, try as they may, to keep the eye in good condition. These would-be defenders of one's eyesight soon bleed into the space in front of the retina, known as the vitreous. And eventually the new vessel growth and the bleeding can cause a detached retina.

Upon examination, an ophthalmologist will find the location of the bleeds soon after they begin, and will end the existence of these determined, well-meaning, but failing do-gooders. When I was first diagnosed with retinopathy almost thirty years ago, the only option was treatment with a laser to destroy the part of the retina that was no longer functioning, so abnormal blood vessels would no longer bleed and the retina would stay attached.

I hoped that would be the end of it—that my vision would be stable—but in Boston, in 1986, one week into out-of-town tryouts for A. R. Gurney's new comedy *Sweet Sue*—Lynn Redgrave was my costar and I was having a great time—disaster struck. It was the first act and Lynn and I were batting the dialogue back and forth when—*wham!*—from the footlights, or follow spot, from nowhere, a crimson dagger was slashing my left eye! And I didn't feel anything. This was a big one—diagonally coursing from the upper corner of the eye to the inside corner. You probably know the old adage "The show must go on." It's seared into the brain of every performer, and despite my conviction that it was uttered by some greedy producer, I credit my fear of what would happen if I interrupted the show with my unshakable determination to lock my knees and remain upright through the end of the scene and completion of Act I.

Robert was in the audience, and when he came to my dressing room I all but jumped him, alternately whimpering and screeching about what had just happened. He immediately got on the phone with Dr. Yannuzzi, the retina specialist. The good Dr. Y arranged for me to see the renowned Lloyd Aiello, M.D., the next morning at Boston's hallowed Joslin Diabetes Clinic. Dr. Aiello, a warm, compassionate man, performed a few emergency stabs with the ol' laser, remarking as he did so that the course of treatment Dr. Yannuzzi had undertaken was excellent, and that this new saboteur was just completing a "farewell tour." Sounded good to me. And though my vision wasn't perfect, at least the dark clouds went away for a good many years.

Since then, the understanding of what is going on inside the eye has progressed enormously, and no one knows more about that than the good doctor himself. So recently I paid Dr. Yannuzzi a visit to find out about the latest developments in diagnosis and treatment.

His office is within a maze of corridors and examining rooms. After all these years, I still can't find his office without help from one of the many staffers, but I do try. As I wended my way to his office without asking someone where I was, I came upon him dashing down another hallway just to my right. Seeing me, he approached, took my hands in his, and said, "Mary, Mary, the 'Bionic Woman.' You look great. I hope the inside does, too. Come this way." Gracefully, he opened a door for me and I responded by catching the toe of my shoe on the carpet. "The old peripheral vision still challenges you, doesn't it?" he asked.

Yes, I answered somewhat testily, and it wouldn't hurt to have some light in here! I've often wondered why an ophthalmologist's office with a waiting room full of people who don't see very well should be so bereft of wattage.

With his bold but charming manner, he sat back in his office chair, relaxed, looking like a man who enjoys his work. "So," he asked, "you want to know about retinopathy today. In some ways you know as much about this complication as anyone could; everything that goes wrong with the diabetic eye was wrong with your eyes. Sit."

I did.

"You had glaucoma, proliferation [growth of abnormal vessels], cataracts, edema, bleeding in the retina. It was angle closure glaucoma and I had to make a hole in each iris to alleviate the pressure."

He never told me I had glaucoma! This was news to me! Did I simply forget that one? I think it's possible that glaucoma escaped my notice, buried as it was in all the other problems and their prognoses. But surely one wouldn't forget the drilling of holes in both eyes!

Dr. Yannuzzi does not pull any punches. Right from the start, he called things as he saw them. With each observation he made of my condition, the news was inescapable. Over time, a small part of me came to resent what I saw as brutality. But as always is the case, I knew I was hearing the truth and I'd much rather see the enemy than blindly thrash about at it.

In our conversation recently his bluntness was undiminished: "You poor lady," he said. "You went through the mill. Shall we talk about what type of person you have been as a patient? At first you were not taking good care of yourself—but you changed and started taking the best care of yourself. I don't know what happened."

I explained that about three years after he first diagnosed my retinopathy I went to the Betty Ford Center and started living like a normal, responsible human being. And I said goodbye to cigarettes. But better living through less chemistry hasn't stopped the deterioration of my vision, alas. I wanted to ask him about my tunnel vision, which makes the world look like a perpetual journey by car through the Swiss Alps.

"First of all," he said, "when the restriction in blood supply takes place in the diabetic eye, it starts in the peripheral retina. That causes you to lose your peripheral vision, and your vision closes into the center. Then when we do laser treatment, we treat the edges of the retina, so it is additive. We're knocking out what little you have there to save your vision so you can read or see theater."

It seems to be getting worse, I said, stupidly hoping for some rebuttal.

Putting his elbows on his desk and leaning forward, he said, "There was an occasion when I had to add a bit of the laser and close in more than I wanted. But before we had laser, if you had proliferation, you had a ninety percent chance of total blindness in five years."

From the blood? I asked.

"Detachment of the retina and bleeding—one of the two mechanisms," he explained. "Diabetic eye disease all happens because of changes in the blood vessels in the body; all over, in the brain, heart, kidneys, the eyes—the microvasculature."

When your ophthalmologist has completed the laser course but there remains the residue of a few more bleeds obstructing your vision, there is surgery called a vitrectomy. It's not something you choose lightly. There have been troublesome outcomes. It involves removing the vitreous (gel) from the front of the retina because it can severely cloud one's vision and provide an excellent culture in which to retain this old and unwanted blood. When it ceases to fade from your vision on its own you must then make a decision. Can you live with it the way it is, knowing it may get worse, or do you opt for this further surgery? Until this development, people who had retinopathy faced the probability of blindness. Diabetes is the leading cause of adult-onset blindness.

Well, thunderclouds were building in my left eye, while the right eye presented an even bigger problem. So, after many conversations with Dr. Yannuzzi and his colleague Dr. Yale Fisher, the vitrectomy specialist, we decided to go ahead. This was 1998.

It was outpatient surgery, but I was fully anesthetized. One of the dangers of this procedure is that during the meticulous process of removing the gel from the retina, the retina itself may become detached from the sclera (the tissue of the eyeball). If this happens, a bubble filled with a combination of gas and air is placed in the eye to hold the retina in position. Most of the eye is made up of brain tissue, which cannot be stitched, necessitating this draconian measure. And because air always rises, the patient must lie facedown, keeping that bubble where it should be. This position must be maintained for most of the hours in the day and night until adherence is achieved. When not prone, one negotiates the trek to the bathroom and back while looking at the floor that lies between the heels. This sentence can last for weeks, during which the seal is made.

I was so happy to be looking at the ceiling when I awakened from the anesthesia!

Prior to my most recent discussion with Dr. Yannuzzi, I had been intrigued by some discussions of a new drug therapy. I asked if there was a new drug treatment and if it would replace laser therapy.

"Yes, but it's used in conjunction with laser. Avastin is a chemotherapy drug we use off label. It is injected into the vitreous, which is the space in front of the retina," he said.

"Cross my heart, hope to die, stick a needle in my eye" floated through my mind. I asked where the injection goes. Where in the eye? Is the Avastin an ongoing treatment or a one-time shot at a cure?

"It's more frightening than painful. We do as little as possible," he said. "Every injection carries a risk—detachment, infection, hemorrhage—but the results are incredible. I recall when Dr. Mort Goldberg and I went down to the FDA to explain why it was necessary to use this group of drugs inside the eye, for example, in 'wet' age-related macular degeneration. We never got to explain it to them because they had done their due diligence and already understood. These injections in the eye are a smaller dose than is used for cancer treatment. But there has never been a clinical trial to support the use of Avastin for retinopathy, or the use of steroids for that matter, either."

But why no test?

"Because it would require a huge number of patients and a sponsor and have to be conducted nationally and at many centers. All eye-care specialists feel it is not necessary to wait for indisputable, clinically driven evidence to use these drugs. It is a decision based on the unanimous opinion of national and international eye-care leaders. The agreement of the people in the field adds up to evidence-driven medicine."

Can the reader go to his or her eye doctor and say, "I want this treatment"?

"No. Ask for an evaluation and then talk with your doctor and make the decision."

My mother-in-law had a few of the injections and didn't think it was enough of an improvement, so she stopped.

"Not everyone sees improvement," Dr. Y explained. "The approved drug that is available for age-related macular degeneration is called Lucentis. Avastin is a kissing cousin of Lucentis. I think Avastin is better for the diabetic and it costs one hundredth of Lucentis. But we don't know for sure which drug works best for macular degeneration or diabetic retinopathy. Clinical trials comparing Avastin and Lucentis for safety and efficacy are under way."

We chatted on for a few minutes, and as I rose to leave he said, "If anything else occurs, please get in touch."

And of course I'll do just that.

9

Diabetes and Dignity

Would that all these incredible advancements in treating retinopathy had been available thirty years ago, when I first developed it. But at the time, laser was the only hope for me. It dramatically improved my vision, but at some costs. Light receptors (rods and cones) are subjected to what might be called "friendly fire." Depending on the amount or severity of the retinopathy, there are trade-offs for treatment. For example, after about twelve or fifteen years of sporadic laser treatment I've noticed a reduction in my ability to see well at night, and this has worsened.

When I'm backstage, for example, or in a dark studio, I may need a friendly hand to guide me over the cables and through the dark corridors of set walls. It's surprising how willing people can be to help and how good at it they are. I haven't found anyone who can help me drive at night, however. But then, I don't drive anymore, so it's not an issue. Another complication is that my color sense is off a little. On St. Patrick's Day, you may see me blithely parading in blue (well, you might catch me strolling, but certainly not blithely). Identifying certain shades of pink from yellow is a baffler, too. But putting questionable colors in specific spots in the closet does the trick, and it appeals to my sense of order, anyway. I'm waiting for the combination of these shades to become hot! Then you'll see some imagination!

I've lost some depth perception, even peripherally. And I must, consequently, try to be aware of what lurks in the shadows of the edges. But these are challenges one can live with.

They provide a few laughs, too. My assistant, Terry, often accompanies me in the city when I go to New York, and as we wend my way through unseen sidewalk surprises (curves, ramps, and the occasional small animal), he prepares me for oncoming assaults. Without missing a beat in his side of the conversation, he heralds the impending threat in a matter-of-fact voice. I'll hear, "curb ahead," "watch that grate," "pavement crack." It's so automatic now that he sometimes does it even when I'm not with him, baffling any companion who has joined him.

But my focal follies are sometimes a challenge to my self-esteem. Dignity . . . diabetes . . . those are two words that should be able to live in the same sentence—and for the most part they do. In fact, it's my mission to make sure that they are never thought of as mutually exclusive: Kids with diabetes can achieve their loftiest dreams. Adults, newly diagnosed with type 2, can reassert their own control over their health. Those of us who have lived with type 1 for decades are able to meet the challenge of emerging complications and continue to optimistically shadowbox with the future. But as someone who is, quite frankly, contending with a roster of diabetes-related deficits, I've discovered that if you add bad lighting, loud noises, and late hours to the mix . . . well, dignity may take a bit of a vacation. You just have to make sure your sense of humor does not.

Case in point: In November 2007 I received a luscious, cream-colored envelope that contained one of those Hollywood invitations I used to wish for when I was a young chorus dancer: "So-and-so [idol] would be thrilled to have you join her [or him] in honoring so-and-so [heavyweight producer] to celebrate such and such's new movie." I say "used to" because while time has increased my ability to gather such invitations, it's also made me realize that I hate these parties.

Why?

The truth is that on some deep subconscious level that won't let go of childhood insecurities, I never feel I'm up to the hipness of my fellow invitees. I know. It sounds ridiculous. But I am woefully insecure, and time has not erased that, apparently. While in the midst of a party of colleagues, I often feel isolated, out of place, and lonely. Everywhere I look there are happy little groups of gorgeous people talking about their current films or the next three that will follow. They don't want me to impose myself into their perfectly orchestrated musical. And so I don't. They somehow know I haven't any project to toss into their center. So Robert and I do Dead Men Walking through the room, carrying on intense, animated conversation with each other while hoping to be rescued by some other misfit before we're identified as being without a country.

But I also have legitimate reasons to be wary of such festive occasions. My hearing is pretty good except that I can't always distinguish the source of a voice in a crowd. I can locate a face to go along with the voice only if the speaker keeps talking while I track an "in-sync" mouth. But add music to that mix, and I become hopeless.

In the din that surrounds a one-on-one conversation, I can only hope that my fellow conversationalist has an expressive face. That way, I can reply with few words and an abundance of mirrored expressions. I get away with it most of the time.

However, on one occasion at a similar party, I blew it big-time! An agent from long ago, who, as I recall, was energetic on my behalf around the time that I put my tap shoes aside for high heels and hoped for the small miracle of an acting assignment, made her way toward Robert and me. She had her sister (a fellow agent) along with her, and after the necessary exchanges there befell on us the dreaded silence. Countering, I graciously asked after their mother. The elder of the duo responded—I did not find out until later when Robert told me—by saying that at age ninety-seven their mother had died of heart failure just a few months prior. What did I say? "Well, please give her a hug for me, and tell her I'll be very upset with her if she doesn't send me her delicious fudge this Christmas."

That's hearing. Can we talk a little more about sight? Because of the retinopathy, I am practically blind in low light, and even when the world is well lit, I have no peripheral vision. Anyone to my side is invisible to me. And if someone proffers a hand at an introduction I may miss it entirely, leaving the would-be acquaintance in a state of mild shock at my seemingly utter indifference.

I worry that people will feel slighted by my obliviousness to their greetings. I can't stand being perceived as aloof. I'm determined to forge through such potential trouble spots and make some of it turn out all right. But I also know that I'll probably have a rough go of it. I just wish I had paid attention to that little voice that told me, "Mary, skip this event!"

To go to this party or not? The envelope from my dear friend Bernadette Peters and actress Glenn Close contained an invitation to a Christmas party for John Travolta's new movie, *Hairspray*. And despite my reflexive resistance, I felt a kinship (Mr. Travolta reminds me of my own beginnings: dancer/actor turned actor/dancer). So how bad could the gathering be, anyway? Well, pretty awful. I don't mean the film and certainly not John in the film.

How to begin? The party was like something out of the Keystone Kops meets the Creature from the Black Lagoon, at least from my point of view. The gathering was held on the third floor of a chic and tough-to-find (aren't they all?) restaurant in New York's theater district. It was so chic that the only illumination was provided by dimly flickering background lights (no brighter than candles) and by, occasionally, tiny blinding spotlights that were sporadically muted by billowing chiffon filling the room and entangling the almost universally black-clad celebrants within it.

There was no elevator, so it was face the stairs. If you'd been there, watching me try to gracefully ascend them, you'd probably assume that I'd had a few before my arrival. But no one was watching me then. What they couldn't have helped but notice later, however, was the way I trod on toes and bumped ever so slightly into other (virtually invisible to me!) guests as I moved through the crowd.

In such situations, it's the way Robert grabs my arm that

provides my only true clue as to how well I am doing or how acute the danger is. If he is content to lead me by the hand, I'm doing pretty well. If he grabs my elbow or waist, I know I am in some peril. And although I depend on and appreciate his watchful protection, it also makes me angry and defensive. I hate that I need someone's help. I resent that diabetes and dignity don't always live so happily in the same sentence. But he persists in looking out for me even though he's risking an ungrateful rebuke. Thank you, Robert, for always putting "Mary the Good" before the "Wicked Witch of the West" that I sometimes am.

On this occasion, the harder it got to negotiate the stairs, the more confusing the lack of adequate light and chaotic the sounds, the more determined I was to prove to myself and others that I could cope. So as people with better vision than I called out to greet me, or occasionally started a conversation, I forged on, confident that Robert's gentle hold on my hand meant all was going well. Spotting Bernadette (well, spotting her hair), I headed up the stairs in her direction, hoping my intrusion into her self-sustaining group would be seen as a friendly addition, not a desperate cry for sanctuary. At the same time, I thought I heard a quasi-familiar voice call to me, and with a half flight of stairs to go, I reached for Robert's hand (in back of me and just to the right) and pushed up against the steadfastly immovable revelers as I searched for "quasi familiar." When that someone called out to me again I turned to face her and we chatted for a minute—I thought. It wasn't until later that I found out I was facing away from her, the side of my head being all she could see, as I chatted easily with the darkness. Heaven knows what she thought of the encounter!

At some point shortly thereafter I lost touch with Robert,

so I reached back and extended my hand, hoping for the connection I needed. Success! As I pulled him through the crowd, something didn't feel right. I turned and was shaken to find . . . a stranger in tow. From what I could gather, he didn't seem to mind. But I let him go anyway.

At this point through my journey in Wonderland, I began to consider that I might be experiencing the beginnings of a low-blood-sugar attack, which can cleverly cloak itself in some of the same symptoms I was feeling: unsteadiness, confusion, feelings of inappropriate nervousness, perspiration, and so on. I don't usually carry blood-testing equipment with me, which would, of course, provide an instant readout of my glucose count. So I covered with a tall glass of orange juice, just in case.

On our way out the door, I spotted Mr. Travolta and waved to him, mouthing a giant thank-you (given my mouth, it was an easy accomplishment). Before I knew it, he'd left his dazzling circle to walk to me. Both his hands were extended and soon encircled mine. He was beaming as he smiled at me and said, "You are a genius." He said that straight to my face! And he voluntarily stepped out of the circle to say it to me. I felt, well, dignified, right with the world, okay.

When we returned home and I could use my monitor, I found my glucose level to be a soaring 250, much too high! One more time with feeling, I guess I needed to learn that lesson again—a quick blood test at the party and I would have known what to do, orange juice or insulin.

All in all, I've learned a lot about myself and about how I underestimate my blood glucose levels, and people, sometimes. And how despite the challenges, with humor, I do believe one can easily couple dignity and diabetes—at least in retrospect.

10

I'm Dancing as Fast as I Can

One of the islands of pleasure and deep satisfaction in my life—my whole life, before and since diabetes—is dancing. My family says I danced before I walked. And as a child, I felt happy dancing, or at the very least, I experienced an absence of fear. Through all the sometimes lonely, jealous, insecure stages of growing up, I had those classes to tell me I was all right. And as an adult, the self-knowledge I gained from dancing led me to see and experience the inevitable outcome of hard work. Discipline makes you better, and even though it doesn't happen overnight, there's no question that growth is occurring. If I had applied the same bone-deep discipline I learned from dance to my sometimes spectacular and sometimes disastrous attempts at controlling diabetes, I might have had a consistently better outcome. It's funny I didn't nail it, because I always knew control was within arm's reach.

Four days a week, from the age of nine until I graduated from high school, I had ballet for forty minutes, tap for thirty minutes, and acrobatics for ten to fifteen minutes, if time and energy allowed. But I figured if it brought me closer to the warm, comforting spotlight that I just knew awaited me, I could summon endless stamina.

In fact, in this one area of my life I was happily confident that I was indeed the keeper of a light, "not to be hidden under a bushel basket." I didn't understand how I was thus rewarded. There was so much about me that missed the mark. But the music and the familiar accomplishments it demanded were strong within me, and if I failed to win Dad's attention with my small triumphs at local USO shows and recitals— "There will come a time, Dad, just you wait and see"—it underscored much of my feelings and thinking.

And years later, during each Friday night filming of *The MTM Show,* didn't I hear his laughter just a second before everyone else's, and a decibel stronger? When I watch reruns, his voice is audible and present.

Who knows at what age I came to understand the word *career.* But once I did I wanted dancing to be mine. Unfortunately, my professional work was limited to chorus dancing on television shows. I never became the star of a ballet company as Moira Shearer had in the movie *The Red Shoes.* Only much later as an actress with my own television show did I experience the indescribable thrill of dancing with Gene Kelly. In 1979 I launched a variety show on CBS. The premise was that I was doing a variety show (in retrospect it doesn't seem as clever a concept as it did at the time!). In that show within a show Gene and I filmed a dance number using the only technique that was acceptable to him—a continuous shoot from beginning to end of the routine. So I had to be flawless. No editing allowed. My recollection is that my feet never touched down during the five days of rehearsal with him—even though I was wearing flats so I wouldn't loom over him.

Dance, especially the training for it, is a big part of me. It shapes the discipline I've brought to my work as an actress, initiated my belief in the adage "No pain, no gain," and generally provided a home that's never changed. No matter what fears assaulted me, as person, actress, or dancer, dance was constantly giving me the familiar steps I needed to grow.

Dance has been my constant best friend.

During the seven years of *The Mary Tyler Moore Show,* I arranged to have three portable ballet barres brought to the soundstage along with a huge mirror on wheels for class. It was a daily lunchtime event, presided over by a woman who'd been my teacher for some twenty years, Sallie Whalen. Music was provided by a classical pianist hired to accompany us on an upright that rolled to our spot in front of the newsroom.

There were usually eight to ten of us—Georgia Engel, Valerie Harper, Beverly Sanders, who played Rayette the waitress on the series, me, and several others who'd once worked as dancers and were now spending their days driving car pools or working as actresses. There were a few young dancers who'd join us from time to time, and when it was over they loved to sit at our dinosaur feet and listen.

It was a touchstone for all of us—sharing the class with its all-too-familiar panting and groaning or sitting on the floor afterward applying bandages to our new blisters.

It was a sisterhood of sorts, not about feminism, but about the nearly religious connection that is ballet class.

I'm often asked where my strength comes from to accept

diabetes and its impingement on my life. I do believe ballet gave me that ability. But it's sad to note that within the successful actress writing this book beats the heart of a failed dancer.

So as I gave up the dream of being a world-famous dancer and became, much to my surprise, a world-famous actress, I clung to dance for pleasure, for structure, and for adventure. Dance took me to places I would never have been privileged to enter without it, and to meet people I revered—and do to this day.

In the late seventies, my agent received a call from a representative of Jacques d'Amboise asking if I would talk to him about a television special he was putting together. *Jacques d'Amboise?!* He wanted to talk to me about a ballet?! When?

There have been some magical people who have touched my life, talented icons with enormous, generous hearts swooping their way into mine. Jacques d'Amboise is one such treasure. If you've been on a cruise for the last fifty years and are unfamiliar with his brilliant career, let me drop a few of his achievements. He was a premier danseur with the New York City Ballet company for decades, starring in ballets such as *Stars and Stripes,* Tchaikovsky's *Pas de Deux, Midsummer Night's Dream, Jewels, Raymonda Variations,* and Brahms's *Schoenberg Quartet,* among others.

M'sieur d'Amboise has had more works that were choreographed for him by George Balanchine (the ballet master of the New York City Ballet) than any other danseur. His reviews were extraordinary, always. Critics and audiences alike have applauded the manliness he brought to the stage, as well as his heart, humor, and mastery of technique. It was arranged that I would see Jacques dance in *Stars and Stripes* in L.A. the following week and we'd talk afterward.

I'd never seen anybody dance the way he dances—so much strength, ebullience, and out-and-out sex appeal. He is one of a kind. When the curtain came down I gathered all of my courage to go backstage as arranged. After I had stood in line for a good half hour while what seemed like half the audience formed an endless line in front of me, my anxiety grew until I was almost unable to speak. From nowhere, he appeared! Taking my hand, he drew me into the dressing room. As with what happened upon my meeting Cary Grant, my end of the ensuing conversation consisted of sounds rather than words. With heartfelt effort, I cleared my throat and said, "Mnsr rshnslv? Dddd dwing nursnge."

Jacques's beautiful wife, Carrie, a talented dancer/choreographer, stood there grinning at me as though she'd seen many versions of apoplexy through the years and understood it for what it was—harmless idolatry. They asked me to come in and sit down, which I did. Over some Perrier, Jacques told me about a ballet he'd been creating with Neil Diamond and the songbook of the late Jerome Kern.

The story was about a woman enthralled with two men, one a dancer with a warm heart, the other a self-centered charmer—a singer. Your guess as to who played whom. Some of the wonderful Jerome Kern music that Jacques planned to use was "The Last Time I Saw Paris," "A Fine Romance," "The Way You Look Tonight," "Smoke Gets in Your Eyes," and many other musical inspirations.

My character was to be the only one who speaks in telling the story; Jacques would only dance and Neil Diamond would be the vocalist.

Unfortunately, for whatever combination of reasons, that project never came to be, but it was the beginning of a long, enduring friendship with Jacques that's allowed me to dance for him in a couple of gala shows for his National Dance Institute (NDI). He founded NDI in 1976 while still a principal dancer at the New York City Ballet. Its goal is to teach children from schools in the tristate area how to learn and perform choreography created by Jacques and his staff. As he has said, "This program, the Event of the Year, is designed to give the experience of participation in an art form, not because I expect the children to become dancers, but so they can experience the magic and the discipline of dance." Everyone (approximately a thousand students from second grade through high school) gathers at Madison Square Garden to rehearse together for the first time, after having practiced at their own schools all year long.

My first participation was in the early eighties; I was a tap-dancing duck leading her young on an exploration of nature. I worked so hard perfecting those taps, making sure they'd be clean and crisp for the performance at the Garden.

We rehearsed at Lincoln Center in its New York State Theater, which is home to the New York City Ballet company. It was a thrill to enter the stage door of that building as though I belonged there with the other dancers who'd be onstage that evening in a serious ballet. I'd show up twice a week to command my feet to remember their schooling from the Ward Sisters' Studio of Dance Arts in Hollywood.

In a rehearsal room set aside for Jacques and company, the beautiful wall of mirrors and meticulously laid sprung wood floors provided a perfect setting for the hard work ahead. It was fun to see the expressions on the faces of members of the corps de ballet who peeked in to see what the racket was that I and the corps de ducks were making.

After a few rehearsals, Jacques and staff came by for a look and smiled their approval of my work. "Thank you," he said.

My hero said thank you to me? He then began to put the kids into the dance. And, oh, they were good—six youngsters ranging in height from four feet to almost six feet tall.

Because Madison Square Garden is a pretty popular venue, especially with athletes, we had no practice on the Garden floor, where we were to give the actual performance, and for our dress rehearsals we were relegated to a small patio outside. We felt good, though, just blocking the movements, with tape on the rehearsal room floor representing the parameters of our space.

On the night of the big show, we performers could be found in small klatches backstage, side stage, wherever there was space, nervously going over our routines, wishing each other good luck, and generally being helpful with anyone needing a broken shoelace replaced. A crying six-year-old who had forgotten to bring her specially chosen Strawberry Pink lipstick was in need of some hugs and convincing that my Misty Rose was just as pretty.

The musicians began their tune-up, which immediately jolted everyone's nerves to a never-expected height, and actions everywhere seemed to be played at fast-forward. It was fascinating to watch these youngsters seemingly take it all in stride, as though the acceleration of their pulses and inability to gulp enough air were appropriate to the situation. They would meet this roaring monster who had taken over head-on!

At the opening, all one thousand children appear onstage, crisscrossing one another, tapping their brains out. It was a stunning feat and led to unending applause.

One ten- or eleven-year-old boy waiting for his entrance stood by me, never taking his eyes off the stage, and kept uttering over and over a breathless "Wow!"

And I think that's exactly what Jacques had hoped for.

About midway through the show, we heard the wondrous singer Judy Collins begin her set. She appears for NDI whenever she can.

The children and I bunched up very close to the proscenium because our musical introduction, "A Walk on the Wild Side," was about to be played, and my duck babies lined up behind me. It was quite some distance to cover, tapping our way to center stage. Because of the welcoming applause, I didn't hear what I didn't hear—*taps!* One could barely make out little clicking sounds, but certainly, there was *no tapping!* It didn't appear to bother my brood, but as I launched into the particular section I'd worked so hard to perfect, there was nothing to be heard. Apparently, the amalgam floor used by the Garden to accommodate the various sports events was going to play no part in this tap dance!

If your feet fail you, keep shaking your little duck butt, and no one will notice. Well, what else are you gonna do? When there's nothing to be done about a bad situation, keep your head up. And here we have a metaphor to illuminate the prior metaphor.

Amazing, isn't it, that while in truth, the whole of the Madison Square Garden floor was at fault, I took the blame on my shoulders? My feet didn't fail me, the floor did. But I didn't see it that way.

Maybe it's not insecurity or humility that compels me to so readily take responsibility for poor results, disappointments, and flaming failures—maybe it's an overwhelming need to be at the center of it all one way or another. Everything depended on me. You see there? Ego! I'd apparently rather have success, but let's not turn our backs on the option of outstanding incompetence!

For another Event of the Year, I was part of a chorus of cops performing a kick line. There was no particular theme or focus for this number. It didn't need any! I was simply one of twelve of New York's finest. I don't know why I was given the honor of being one of them, unless it was to keep them honest! I was introduced as being third from the right and that's as it should have been, nice and simple. Those "fine ones" were the big attraction. They worked so hard to please Jacques. And didn't they just! Well, we brought the house down.

It's a grand experience full of laughs and admiration for the children, who bring with them not only a sense of accomplishment, but also joy at having done it all.

Joy in accomplishment, even if imperfect, is a lesson that people have been trying to teach me—and I've been trying to learn—in one way or another all my life. And Jacques, with his generous spirit, his talent and humor, is an ongoing source of wisdom and wit.

Recently I sat and talked with him in my home, recalling the adventures of dancing in Balanchine's class, an honor that Jacques arranged for me. Jacques's impression of Balanchine, the motions of his head and his staccato (and whispered) way of speaking, put me right back into his class. Standing at the barre, feeling nervous, chewing gum (I thought rather discreetly), which I hoped would address the dehydration that a diabetic may experience. A dry mouth can also be made drier by tension. Well, this was a class under the tutelage of the master, George Balanchine, and the pressure I felt was high. I wasn't auditioning for a place in the company, for heaven's sake, but I was enjoying the honor of having been invited to participate while trying to keep my tongue from adhering to my teeth.

My sculpture of George Balanchine would be that of a rather short, sleek silver missile. He spoke in an almost whisper, causing all in the class (about twenty-five people) to summon absolute silence as he gave each direction.

From childhood, I had been taught that gum chewing was frowned upon, unacceptable behavior for a young lady. So, imagine my shock and feelings of dishonor when Jacques quoted Mr. B's unexpected review of my participation in his class: "She did well, but she was chewing gum voraciously with every count. Every *tendu* there was a chew, followed by another and another when we did battements. You should tell her it's not a good idea to chew gum. She could swallow it and . . . ask her not to chew gum."

And Jacques told Balanchine, "You know she has diabetes. . . ."

Mr. B said, "Okay, okay. Tell her not to breathe . . . because sometimes you gasp in when you execute a dance step and if you have gum in your mouth, it could go into your lung. . . . Be careful not to breathe!"

Despite my (literal and figurative) faux pas, Mr. Balanchine asked for a "sit-down" the following day. He had created a new ballet and wanted to talk it over. We met at the Empire Coffee Shop across the street from Lincoln Center. As the three of us—Mr. B, Jacques, and I—wended our way through the hustle-bustle, schmooze hub that was the Empire Coffee Shop, I became aware of the lowering of volume that met our progress toward the only empty table in the room—Mr. B's.

The patrons were made up of excruciatingly young dancers, reedy old men with long white hair, matrons of the arts, and executive types seated with creatively dressed young men.

Every head was either turned toward us or facing one another directly while only their eyes followed us. It made me feel like one of the trio of Furies in an oddly cast Greek tragedy. Yes—the casting!

What could these three be about?

Here's what.

Mr. B had a loosely drawn concept for a prequel to *The Nutcracker Suite* ballet. He thought I'd be interested in doing it as a television special. But since, aside from that one gum-chewing class, he'd never seen me dance full-out, had he put the ol' horse before the cart? Shouldn't he talk to Grant about producing this project? And then cast it with a strong dancer? I think that's what he probably had hoped for from the start.

I called Grant and relayed to him my meeting with Mr. B. "Mr. *What?*" he said.

Balanchine, I responded. He wants to choreograph this story for TV. And I told him the outline.

"Is this something you want to do?"

Oh, Grant, I wailed, this man is the master choreographer of the century. What an opportunity! But I don't know if I'm good enough to dance it. I haven't been on pointe in years and I don't know what to do.

"I think you do," he offered, "and, Mary, I wouldn't know what to do with it anyway."

It all just evaporated in time. The B man didn't ask and I didn't tell. But Grant did. Apparently he told Mr. B that it sounded beautiful, but just wasn't within his bailiwick. "Where is Bailiwick located?" George Balanchine asked him. Grant didn't tell.

Jacques confided an aspect of Mr. B that few know about. He was a "ladies' man," married a few times, and in love with ballerinas almost exclusively. He was fascinated by athleticism in women and, according to Jacques, had a seven-foot color cutout of Lynda Carter as Wonder Woman on the back of his bathroom door at the theater. *The MTM Show* was a favorite of his, and he apparently referred to me as "Ah, yes, the American Filly."

If only I'd known some of this before I'd taken that nerve-wracking first class watching him watch me chew gum.

In the years since then, dance has stayed center stage in my heart—and in 2004 Dick Van Dyke and I did a wonderful reunion show, *The Dick Van Dyke Show Revisited,* which was produced and written by Carl Reiner with writers Bill Persky and Sam Denoff on call. It brought us up-to-date with Rob, now retired, and Laura (me) teaching ballet classes to our granddaughter and the neighborhood denizens. In one scene that Carl had specially written for me, I'm shown demonstrating how I want the children to execute the steps I've just shown them.

Before we began rehearsals for the show, I worried that I might be a bit rusty and no longer able to do the dancing required. I hadn't taken a class for a few years and, as a result, I bumped smack into the consequences! I was shocked and frightened when David Howard, the choreographer, gave me a few pirouettes to do and *I was unable to carry them out!* On my first try, the walls moved dizzyingly. I tried again, only to find the floor moving up to meet me as well. Okay, let's try another kind of turn. My favorite—*chaînés* across the floor, never stopping. But this time I had to! I was falling to the ground.

The scene worked just fine without the elusive pirouettes, but my balance was off some, too, leaving me feeling like a bird who could no longer fly. Only another dancer would notice the absence, I think.

While I still must deal with flawed balance and curbs that surprise me, my heartbreak of that afternoon is mending. After all, I'm seventy-two years old, and to quote Dr. Yannuzzi, I'm something of a "Bionic Woman." I'll settle for that.

I've become intrigued lately with an old form of exercise that is being newly promoted, though there are few teachers who are truly qualified to teach it. A man named Joseph Pilates devised it on his own in the 1930s. (Balanchine was a student.) It involves the use of a padded bench on which you lie with feet and/or hands pumping these hand and foot straps. They're attached to what looks like a trapeze, which when it painfully stretches your body gives specific muscles—and at the same time overall postural muscles—a good workout. A Pilates class is mild torture, challenging, yet non-sweatifying—you just don't do very much. An aspect of this form of exercise that I like is that because you are prone, there's no mirror to tell you how far off the mark you are. It's just you, your progress, and your instructor. As with anything, though, you've got to have a knowledgeable instructor, not a health club prancer who's merely watched a class or two and considers him- or herself to be qualified.

I augment this strength training with cardiovascular workouts three or four times a week, during which I use the treadmill, rowing machine, and the elliptical cross-trainer. Each form of exercise relies not at all on vision or balance, which are no longer my strong points after all these years of diabetes—and, well, age. Yes, that too.

These days, I exercise in ways that don't require much artistry, sad to say. And I do miss the classical music of ballet.

Now I just throw myself to the mat making little fists while humming through clenched teeth "I Won't Dance, Don't Ask Me."

11

The Other Element

As I have said, dance forms the basis of who I am. It has filled my life with a sense of purpose and of transcendence—it anchored me and lifted me up. It made me aware of who I am and put me in a greater context as part of the amazing society of those who know how to speak not just with words but with actions.

Another essential element in my life that continues to shape my sense of love, of connection, and of the universal majesty of life is my interaction with animals. Sometimes I feel like my dogs—particularly my pit bull, Spanky—know me better than I know myself.

There have been countless reports of the great benefits that come from animal interactions with people, particularly sick people. The animals' help can result from something as simple as their being in the same room or lying on a patient's bed with them. Dogs in particular seem to be endowed with remarkable sensitivity in vision, hearing, taste, smell, and touch. (Pigs also rank at the top of the list, but because they are farm animals, we're not always inclined to use them as helpers to ailing people.)

For a long time, I've been aware that dogs can react to high or low blood sugars in people and then alert the person or a caregiver that something is amiss. Spanky does that for me. He follows me around the house as my glucose level begins to change—long before I am aware that something is up. Once I alight somewhere, he sits in front of me, staring at me until I get the message. My other three dogs (Shadow, a nine-year-old golden retriever, Shana, an eight-year-old miniature schnauzer, and James, a three-year-old Petit Basset Griffon Vendéen) may glance at me from time to time, but seldom, if ever, with the intensity of our pit, Spanky. I think in animals such as Spanky there exists an extra sense—is it ESP? These animals have the inarguable ability to read their guardian's or special person's state of being and state of mind. The Delta Society, a wonderful national organization that organizes and brings animals to hospitals for hands-on visitations with a wide variety of patients, employs dogs, cats, and even pigs.

Animals' uncanny ability to communicate with humans is not the only thing they share with us, unfortunately. Animals develop diabetes, too (did you know?), though not in the numbers we do.

Long before I joined the ranks of the diagnosed, my then-six-year-old gray miniature poodle, Maude, began to lose her appetite, drank more than usual, and became lethargic, all unrecognizable symptoms to me. Her brother, Max, a nine-ish-year-old German shepherd who'd been her guide through puppyhood, showing her the magic of shrubs, tall grasses, flower beds (oh, yes, flowers!), was her playmate and sleeping companion and had taken (of late) to watching her closely. And so I did, also. What I noticed was that she didn't play with him now. No more fake snarling, stealing each other's toys, or engaging in territorial discussions. Maude was a feisty little thing. She ruled. But when Max had had enough, he'd roll her on her back, taking her whole head in his mouth and holding it there as if to say, "Just remember what I could do to you if I chose."

I wish I'd seen earlier that Maude was sick and not just in a mood. Dogs can fool you that way. They're so stoic.

After finally figuring out that our vet ought to have a look, we took her in for tests. That afternoon he reported that her kidneys were failing and said he'd do whatever he could, but not to expect much. She had diabetes. I'd had just a vague notion of what that was. Leaving her there, we went home and gave Max extra hugs and tried to anesthetize the crippling ache in our throats. We visited Maude for two days, watching her fade, then witnessing certain improvement, and then seeing her eyes sink even deeper into that dear face. On the third night at three A.M., the phone rang, and before I could answer it, of course, I knew who it was. The voice said, "If you want to say good-bye, this would be the time."

She must have known we were there because she was lying on her side with her eyes closed, but when I whispered her name she lifted her head with great effort, then put it down again.

There now exist treatments that owners can administer to animals with diabetes before it's too late. It's not as successful as treating people, but we're going to have a cure some day for us all. A cure.

Knowing how I love animals—all life, really—I'm sometimes asked how I reconcile myself to the animal experimentation of science. Naturally I feel awful about it. They're so vulnerable. I can't even watch a film that shows the circle of life, as natural as it is (prey and predator), every one of them seeking sustenance at the gruesome death of another.

While in Africa I watched from a Range Rover as a mother and baby gazelle enjoyed the sun and grazed on the Masai Mara, unaware of the lioness watching from nearby. It was the video we've all seen of just this situation, only now it was real. Oh no, God, no! Don't let it happen. The predator, still watchful, just then lay down, seemingly having changed her mind as if in answer to my angry prayer. I thought the heart-pounding danger would vanish behind the rocks that had hidden her to begin with. But so quickly, she rose again and tore across the flat, hard land. Dust was being kicked up, making it difficult to see. Maybe that was a blessing. But somehow she'd separated the two gazelles and chased the youngster as if in play while the mother charged and withdrew, then raced back and forth. Then came the scream. Just one from the babe. What I'll never be able to erase from my memory is the mournful bleating of the mother. We could hear her for a long time.

As long as science is respectful of animals, not replicating experiments when unnecessary, caring for as well as using them (they also have an emotional connection), I can live with it.

There exists within JDRF a conscious effort to fund those projects that will lead to animal experiments becoming a thing of the past. We call it "Bench to Bedside," wherein trials use humans as test subjects instead of animals, which often yield scientific results that differ from those that people would provide. So, on two levels, it's a step forward.

Dogs have not been my only close relationships with animals. I have long loved horses as well. So after living at the San Remo Apartments on Central Park West, Robert and I and our growing golden retriever needed some more space. We concluded that a small country house would add some yin to the yang in all three of us. We never thought of moving out of New York entirely, just buying some grass that we could nurture on weekends while watching our dog drop his city duds and run naked.

Lots of looking and talking about what we were looking for finally produced Greenawn, a twenty-one-acre property with a house and gardener's cottage, three ponds, and a brook gracefully etching its way from one pond to the next and then off to unseen neighboring farms.

It impelled us to fence a small meadow, creating a paddock for two or three horses, and of course, to build a small barn and groom's apartment to keep everybody well schooled and cared for. Needless to say, "small" led to "large" in no time as we considered all possibilities. What if a couple came for a hack (trail ride)? We'd be missing a steed. But add another stall, and then wouldn't it be grand to mate my Palomino with another, producing a golden quarter horse foal?

The birth of that colt was a near-religious experience. He was born in the middle of the night and I watched every minute of it. Fanny, our mare, did everything right in getting John (named for my brother) to his wobbly feet. Oh my, was he gorgeous! Great bones, handsome face, and the palest Palomino I'd ever seen. He was white! And . . . he had blue eyes! He came from twice-vetted Palominos (both parents and grandparents) with some obviously strong throwback gene that only added to his beauty. When he was reticent to suckle, my girl insisted. She nursed him like she was born to the task, played with him, never letting him out of sight.

One day as I watched them, Fanny, who seemed to be feeling like she could do anything—trotting, then screeching on her brakes, attempting what appeared to be a balletic *tour en l'air*—dropped to her knees, lowered her hindquarters, and rolled to her back for some good ol' (feet held high) belly scratching. She was in horse heaven when her two-week-old son, John, seemingly terrified, raced to her and jumped over her belly, causing an entanglement of eight legs as they struggled to recover.

It was all happening so quickly, but within that time, I was, of course, able to imagine in detail all the horrid possibilities for an outcome. This is a self-defense method I created at a young age to protect myself from surprises and catastrophes. The theory (game) is that if I can conjure the unbearable before it becomes a fact, then "It won't happen at all, you silly!" And all, indeed, was well.

So Robert and I continued for some time to enjoy our seesaw between city and country. We moved to the east side of Central Park (something that West Siders say requires a visa) and found that our urban life was to be enhanced—at least initially—by a most unexpected arrival.

One day, a few years after the move to the Fifth Avenue apartment, I became aware of something new—a small group, maybe five or ten people, on the sidewalk looking up at my living room window. Some were pointing and taking pictures, sharing binoculars, all with great animation. It was as though they'd come upon the resting place of the Holy Grail.

I hid myself as best I could behind the window treatment (a term I'd picked up from my interior designer—"We don't say drapery, and never, certainly, drapes. It's called a window treatment"). Well, I'd chosen shades, so my cover was difficult if not an out-and-out impossibility. You can't drape yourself in shades.

But I had to know what was going on, so I took the elevator to the lobby, where I sidled over to George, our doorman, and asked if he had heard anything in the building. Had there been something about me in the papers? I was most apologetic for the group, which was perfectly ruly, by the way, but I had been told by the president of the building's board when he finally agreed to let us buy our apartment that I was "an exception to their position regarding 'members of the *entertainment force.*'" He had said: "We're very quiet here, Miss Moore. No loud parties or spectacles."

My father had always taken great pride in the ancestry of the Moores, pointing out their involvement in the Revolutionary and Civil Wars. He would describe our family as being the "descendents of impoverished nobility." I have portraits of them all. So the superior tone of *Monsieur le Président*'s unnecessary caution rankled me.

I think it was the reverence that people have for doctors that gained us entry, finally. I'd been well behaved there for several years, but here this was, a *spectacle* being conducted at our front door.

"Mrs. Levine," George reassured me, "everyone is pleased to have you here in our building, but this has nothing to do with you. This group and others have come to see the nest of hawks on the grillwork outside the twelfth-floor window."

The hawks had recently laid three eggs, as they had each spring for a few years. "You didn't cause the attention," he said.

It's extraordinary that this family of hawks had chosen to make its home not in any one of the magnificent trees in the park, but on the sheer stone cliff that is 927 Fifth Avenue!

I'd noticed the rare droppings on the sidewalk, but hawks are scrupulous about not leaving evidence of their nesting for fear a fellow predator might find them. What few droppings they'd overlooked, our dear doormen were quickly there to clear away any trace of their existence.

Over the next few days I asked some sidewalk people for any more details they could give me. Two of the people who were most informed, yet still giddy with excitement, were author Marie Winn, who has since written two books on the subject, the first being *Red-Tails in Love: A Wildlife Drama in Central Park* followed by *Central Park in the Dark,* and an award-winning photographer of great heart and much talent, Lincoln Karim. He showed me some breathtaking shots he'd taken over time of Pale Male and his mate, Lola (names assigned them by their fans), and their fledglings in all stages of development. There were stunning images of the master progenitor. And I tell you, I saw majesty in the aristocratic angle of his head, the piercing focus of his eyes. In his fourteen years to date, Pale Male has spawned twenty-three fledglings, most of whom are still living in the vicinity.

I was eventually to become a full-fledged member of the sidewalk people's cult, some of whom were members of the Audubon Society. Several times a week I would join them and peer through Lincoln's gigantic lens to track the fledging of those first babies as well as the many that followed.

Top: The first of many musical numbers on *The Dick Van Dyke Show*—"I am a fine musician." *(Courtesy of CBS)*

Left: Dick Van Dyke and Mary Tyler Moore meet Laurel and Hardy. *(Courtesy of Annie Leibovitz)*

In later life, Elvis said, "I've slept with all my leading ladies, except one."
I don't want to blow anyone's cover, but I *know* who the one is.
And what was I thinking!
(Courtesy of Universal Studios Licensing LLLP)

A secret night visitor—the late Dudley.
(Courtesy of Mary Tyler Moore)

First Lady Betty Ford, in a boffo "cameo" on our show.
(Courtesy of the Gerald R. Ford Library)

With lovable Lucy, whose early "Kid, you've got talent"
filled my veins with belief in her judgment.
(Courtesy of CBS)

Back to the chorus with Jacques d'Amboise!
(Courtesy of Carolyn George)

Gavin, where are you?
(Courtesy of Craig T. Mathew/Mathew Imaging)

Top: Surrounded by angels at JDRF's Children's Congress.
(Photo courtesy of The Juvenile Diabetes Research Foundation.
Photographer: Larry Lettera, Camera One)

Left: Oh, how I loved him! And still do.
(Courtesy of CBS)

Right: Just minutes before this picture was taken, Robert and I had a
world-class fight! Love conquers all.
(Photo courtesy of The Juvenile Diabetes Research Foundation.
Photographer: Larry Lettera, Camera One)

Top: Rallying the troops for a JDRF walk.
(Photo courtesy of The Juvenile Diabetes Research Foundation. Photographer: Larry Lettera, Camera One)

Center: A hero of mine and JDRF's as well, Newt Gingrich.
(Photo courtesy of The Juvenile Diabetes Research Foundation. Photographer: Larry Lettera, Camera One)

Left: Another hero of mine—Pale Male.
(Courtesy of Lincoln Karim)

Let's walk across the Brooklyn Bridge for JDRF and a cure.
*(Photo courtesy of The Juvenile Diabetes Research Foundation.
Photographer: Larry Lettera, Camera One)*

My elusive dad, yet always in my heart.
(Courtesy of Mary Tyler Moore)

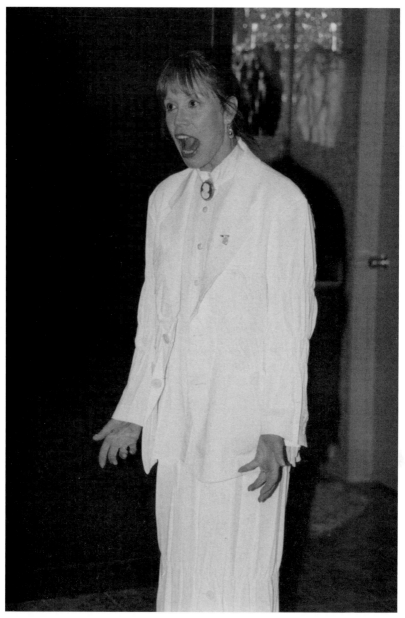

If I see one more picture of her, I'm going to scream!
(Courtesy of Mary Tyler Moore)

Early one morning, several months later, I got a phone call from a sobbing Lincoln Karim, who related, as best he could, a horror story that had taken place the night before.

Apparently two men had descended from the roof of our building on scaffolding and summarily torn apart the temporarily empty nest, hurling it into the back of their truck before driving off, leaving the sidewalk in front of 927 Fifth Avenue with a scattering of a few broken twigs, horsehair, and feathers. What a good night's work, gentlemen!

There had been rumors of unscheduled meetings of the board having taken place to discuss the "hawk issue," but it never occurred to anyone that they would take such violent action. As I stood there on Fifth Avenue looking up at the goneness of that nest, I was nearly overwhelmed with shivering anger. I looked to the sky and then that emotion became shadowed by the sudden sight of Pale Male tracing circles over the building. He carried a stick in his mouth, and it broke my heart to see him in what appeared to me to be a frantic and doomed attempt to make it right again. That vision clawed at my throat and chest in exquisite recollection of a prior grief.

Their nest was torn down in darkness to avoid any protests. Had I known, I would have led those protests with no self-restrictions. It wouldn't be the first time I'd "lost it" in defense of a mistreated animal.

As the days wore on, our crowd grew, some three hundred people at times, resulting from the television and newspaper coverage. We stood determinedly on the sidewalk, carrying large placards that read, HONK IF YOU CARE ABOUT THE HAWKS.

Before long, the majority of automobiles began responding with the blaring of horns. I'm talking about buses, taxis, trucks, police cruisers, all showing their displeasure at what had happened to those creatures. So, adding to the humiliation the board had to endure from the press was the irritation of the board's president, who lived on the second floor of our building and now was enduring several days of incessant, inescapable honking by an irate New York City.

It may not have been the only reason, but the wrenching trauma of Pale Male's eviction from our apartment building coincided with an increase in the country's lure, and Robert and I decided to sell the Fifth Avenue apartment and have done with the city's incessant honking, traffic dead ends, evicted red-tailed hawks, crumbling streets, and mean-spirited neighbors.

Back at Greenawn, we eventually acquired more contiguous land (150 acres now), which begged to be inhabited by more and more rescue horses and two goats. There were two retired police mounts and two Premarin foals that needed rescuing from inhumane treatment in manufacturing birth control medication.

They gave us such pleasure as we rode them on our tree-shaded hilly trails and through golden meadows with views of the Catskill Mountains (home of some exquisitely funny comedians).

My declining vision soon made it too dangerous for me to ride. Robert loved to ride his enormous Clydesdale Thoroughbred, Dozer (as in "Bull"), but he lost interest without a buddy to accompany him (a person, not another horse; another person on a horse—not his, of course, of course).

The very small town that once felt very cozy began to pale. It was lovely and bucolic as a part-time escape from the city, but living in the country full-time meant an hour and a half's drive to my doctors and shopping, etc., and it began to bring stress of another sort into my life experience.

I can no longer drive due to those vision limitations, and that, too, made me pine for the old city life that allowed me to pop around the corner by foot to Madison Avenue for some "look-sees." I wanted to reestablish the relationship I'd built over the years with our dry cleaner, who picked up and delivered clothes that looked fresher and newer than when I'd first bought them. There is no dry cleaner at all in the small nearby town of Millbrook. But then I was wearing exercise clothes and jeans most of the time, anyway. The truth is, we'd overcomplicated our lives with activities that couldn't be enjoyed anymore and which, at the same time, inflicted some isolation.

So we found loving homes for all of the horses and moved into a more suburban environment in Connecticut, where hawks still coast overhead occasionally, and the dogs can frolic in a big enclosed yard, but city conveniences are close at hand. Our resettled nest seems a perfect resting spot, suited to all of our sometimes conflicting needs and impulses.

For Pale Male and his mate, Lola, unfortunately, the resettling process has not been so smooth. After pressure from the Audubon Society and the press coverage, the apartment building owners on Fifth Avenue were persuaded to construct an iron cradle for the hawks, where it was hoped they would rebuild their nest. And they did, in time. The loving pair has added to it every spring since the outrage, and each spring Lola has laid three eggs and sat faithfully on them. None has hatched.

When we value our own convenience more than the balance and beauty in the world, we pay a price. We may eliminate

bird droppings on our sidewalk, but we leave our skies empty
of the beauty that a soaring hawk bestows.

A poet named Matthew Sperling wrote this and sent it to me.

The Nest of a Hawk

Every time you lift your hand against magic,
Against the unexplained, against the beautiful,
You endanger what is and what will be,
Just as you do if you try to throw away the jewel
Joined to that sometimes cloudy strand of blue.
If you destroy the nest of a hawk
In the middle of New York City,
A nest on the ledge of a building,
A nest that should not be there
Twelve stories above the concrete,
Softly lined with feathers and
The pelts of unlucky rats,
A hawk's place, a launching pad
That has survived for eleven years
With traffic crawling below,
With so many people flattened
By being at the height of civilization,
Staggering under the need to catch
A cab, a bus, a subway, a limo, a helicopter,
All those devices we depend on to lift us,
To speed us like a hawk
Wings spread as it drifts in the currents,
That height of nothingness where there is

Only sky, only clouds, only sunlight,
Only a place for the moon to grow and disappear
After it has shined on
The nests of hawks and of men and women
Praying, even those who do not know how,
For some magic to save them
From so many certainties and so much power.
We can pray for power,
Yet our prayer will be incomplete
Unless we also pray
To use our power wisely.

12

Owning Diabetes

It took me years and years to get to the point where I could announce to the world, "I am Mary Tyler Moore, and I have diabetes." But announce it I did in 1984, when I agreed to become the international chairman of the Juvenile Diabetes Foundation. I'd already made a couple of public service announcements on television asking for donations to JDF, but the spots said nothing about my also being a diabetic. I felt virtuous and yet protected from public scrutiny of my disease. But JDF (now JDRF) was and is a remarkable foundation, made up of a staff and volunteers, which allows the organization to give more than 85 percent of its funds to support scientific research and research-related education. It annually receives top rankings from independent sources that rate charities. So I was honored to be asked to affiliate myself with them and their serious work funding medical research.

It all happened when Gloria Pennington, the newly appointed executive director, sat me down (it was on the set of some show) and made her persuasive pitch. Sipping tea for two, we chatted about the latest findings in the disease, office gossip (never anything good there), and then—"Mary, would you consider becoming the international chairman of JDF? We've done some testing on how people feel about you, and apparently they trust you. You are a diabetic and they believe what you say and admire how you've conducted your life. The board of directors has met and unanimously agreed that you're the right person."

With terror coursing through my veins, I pressed my knees together in an attempt to stop their shaking. What would I do as this, ah . . . person? I remember asking her.

She replied, "We'd like you to go to Washington, D.C., from time to time to ask for increased funding from the government and talk to Congress and Senators about how much this disease is costing. [It was $132 billion in 2002. This included a doubling of the direct costs from $44 billion to $91.8 billion.] If you're available, we'd ask you to attend a few fundraising dinners. We'd like you to make more public-service television spots, but now as chairman you'd relate that you, too, are a person with juvenile diabetes."

I wasn't keeping it a secret exactly. It just wasn't as widely known as it would be after I made a statement like that! *A statement?* Well, I mean, you don't just mention something like that.

I have to admit, Gloria's request caused the MTM smile to contort a bit, but for reasons you might not guess. My mind was clicking with these questions: If I tell the public that I have diabetes, won't they say to themselves, "Well, it can't be all that serious a disease. Look at her, she's energetic, bursting with health, never sick! There are much worse diseases than diabetes." The other end of the seesaw (do they still have those?) was my fear that as the public watched me acting my brains out they would be thinking, "Oh, it's sad she has diabetes and, from what I hear, there is no cure for it."

JDF could take a bad blow from the first scenario, and I wouldn't like the second one even a bit.

I finally put a stop to my ambivalence by thinking, "Just do what you know is right, stupid." (There she was again—annoying, but right).

It wouldn't be my first time testifying before Congress. The first time I went with Gloria (Steinem, not Pennington) and her colleagues (Bella Abzug, Gloria Allred, Shirley Chisholm, and other heat-packing defenders of feminism) to fight for the passage of the Equal Rights Amendment.

Gloria Steinem felt we should keep the pressure on Congress to right this wrong. So, relying on the character that was Mary Richards, they responded to a comment of then Speaker of the House of Representatives Tip O'Neill that, "Yes," he would keep in mind the equality of women, or lack of it, in the workplace, and look forward to the next visit. "Oh, and would Mary Tyler Moore be coming, too?" "Well, of course she would, Mr. Speaker."

Within weeks, there I sat in the Speaker's office, nervously clutching my prepared "sales pitch" and silently exchanging encouraging smiles with my accompanying posse. And there he was suddenly! A great hulking presence wearing a beret of white hair, bellowing as he entered, "Where is she? Ah, there's that little cutie. Well, come over here and give your papa bear a big hug." *Tip O'Neill?* It turned out that there was no opportunity for me to speak, yet they all assured me that I'd made a major impact. After all, Mary Richards was the epitome of feminism, wasn't she? How odd that the trotting out of a "little cutie" contributed to bra-burning feminism.

But there is something fundamentally different about my relationship with JDRF. We have something very personal in common, and though I would not have been able to recite the ERA, I certainly know what it means to live with diabetes. And that's basically what JDRF wanted me to share with Senators and House members.

The first time I headed to the Hill for JDRF, I remember wondering if I should wear my eyeglasses so I could read my testimony better, or would I look less ill without them. But maybe if I looked less ill, we'd lose the impact of how serious diabetes really is. So here I was back on the merry-go-round of wanting to look hearty but not too hearty. And as to that lack of self-confidence, all I had to do is remember Spencer Tracy's answer when asked the secret of his success: "Show up on time, hit your marks, and tell the truth."

Now, after many years of interaction with Congress, I've come to understand better the difference between the political hug and knowledgeable advocacy. It feels like success—and it works.

In my early visits and testimony, JDF was a very small organization. In our war chest we'd collected enough money to turn over to research between $8 and $10 million a year (we now give approximately $200 million a year). Sure, we had a D.C.-based law firm helping us out (mostly pro bono) and we had good relationships on the Hill dating from our founding "moms'" early efforts to get Congress to recognize the need for more diabetes research.

Today, we've not only added another letter to our name—R for research—but we've become a partner with government. We can say to those on the Hill, "We're not asking for a handout as we search for the cure; we're your partners. And we're every bit as determined as those founding moms."

Every other year, a group of one hundred to two hundred children representing the fifty states is brought together by JDRF in Washington, D.C., to tell Congress their personal stories of living with diabetes and to ask, as I do, that more money be given to research for a cure. They spend two and a half days visiting the Hill, speaking both formally in the Senate hearing room as well as individually to the representatives in their offices as Little Advocates.

Some of the time is spent as a group getting to know one another. At the welcoming dinner, I ask each of the children to stand and introduce him- or herself, giving his or her state and age. They often range from three to eighteen years old, and a finer bunch of kids you'd have trouble collecting. "I'm Stewart Slatterly from Texas and I'm nine years old." "I'm Nancy Brown from California and I am six years old." "I'm Mia—I wanna pee." And so it went—really, that's a quote! Finally, it was my turn. "I'm Mary Tyler Moore from New York and I'm sixty-two years old."

Can you imagine the tension these brave young visitors must feel on Capitol Hill in Washington, D.C., where the laws we live by are made? The houses and offices of our country's history. The huge American flags everywhere you look! Why, it makes you feel that losing the last soccer game wasn't the worst thing ever. This is the worst thing ever: having to talk to these very important people. I'm not smart. Maybe I'll wreck everything.

But I love talking to these kids, answering their questions, hearing their triumphs, their fears, and about Laura's new boyfriend who isn't diabetic. They give me the gift of friendship and support. Because they share their stories with me, I am able to witness the courage of our children with type 1, and I find new strength to face my own day-to-day challenges of life with diabetes.

Mollie and Jackie Singer are nineteen-year-old twins; Mollie has had diabetes since the age of four, and Jackie does not have it. These talented and beautiful girls (they are headed to Nashville to see about advancing their singing careers) were born three months prematurely, but recovered and have gone on to achieve remarkable things in their nineteen years on earth. At the age of eight, the girls started a group called Diabetic Angels (diabeticangels.com), which has spread around the world. They formed the first chapter in Las Vegas after one too many mortifying incidents at the girls' school. The last straw was when Mollie was "uninvited" to another child's birthday party because "diabetics are a hassle." Mollie was humiliated and hurt, but with Jackie's support, she vowed to educate her peers and prevent other children from experiencing such hurtful episodes. And the two of them have been very active in JDRF. To date they have raised more than $500,000 for research through their various activities. "We raise funds," they told me, "through the Walk to Cure Diabetes, letter-writing campaigns, JDRF galas, and getting people online to make donations, and asking people to donate online through our Web sites, and our MySpace and YouTube sites."

But their beguiling sweetness and in-your-face toughness were yet to be in evidence when I first met them. The way they tell it, they were feeling pretty isolated and unhappy in 1999 when they went to the Children's Congress in Washington, D.C., to help me lobby our representatives for more research funding.

Says Mollie: "We were just kids, and it was overwhelming to be there walking the hall of Congress with you, Mary. It was. And meeting a lot of other kids who had diabetes meant so much. When I was first diagnosed there was no one for me to talk to. I didn't know anyone else who had diabetes. When Jackie and I finally came to the Children's Congress there were a hundred kids with diabetes and so many adults."

"The government officials that we spoke to really cared about what we had to say," adds Jackie.

"And," says Mollie, "the chance to testify with Mary Tyler Moore, well, we were overcome with emotion. Mary, you are one of our heroes. You showed us how to be strong."

Over the years I've had so many people, youngsters and adults, thank me for "doing what you do." But no one can know how much it does for me! The effort is my gift to myself.

When I first joined JDF, we were small, but we were no less influential. The passion of our families, who would invite future giants of diabetes research to dinner, came through clearly—shaping these young scientists' thinking and animating their pursuit of research solutions. Many of the advances we are seeing today had their germination in the relationships that were built back then.

One of the most special parts of my work with JDRF is the partnership that Robert and I formed to help the organization mature and flourish. He had dedicated countless hours and days and months and years to helping the organization and supporting my role as well. I know he misses "hands-on" medicine, but his contributions to JDRF are vital. He has, over the years, provided the organization with informed medical experience, coupled with the overall brain power resting beneath that lush, curly black hair I found so attractive twenty-five years ago. Not bad now, either.

In 1989, Robert was appointed to the JDF International Board to the seat vacated when David Dinkins was elected Mayor of New York City. (An aside: Mayor Dinkins, in 1983, when he was City Clerk, issued the marriage license that allowed me to add the Levine to Mary Tyler Moore. But wait, let's be honest here: My true name is Mary Tyler Moore Meeker Tinker Levine.)

Back to Robert. In 1994, he drafted the report to the board developing the case for a focus on support for "Bench to Bedside" initiatives. A year later, he developed the overarching concept of "Path to a Cure" to help the JDF board and constituencies understand the challenges of finding a cure and the steps along the path. "Path to a Cure" led to a fundamental change in the approach to research funding, as well as to the creation of critical research resources to accelerate progress.

In 2005, Robert developed a vision of idealized "Clinical Practice Guidelines" to help the board understand the types of diagnostic and treatment programs that were conceivable if the now renamed organization—the Juvenile Diabetes Research Foundation (JDRF)—were to be successful in its research programs.

We launched our first major donor initiative, "The Only Remedy Is a Cure" campaign, in 1990. We were unsure if we could raise $100 million in ten years. Of course we did it in fewer than five, and now we raise more than $200 million each year. Then in 1995, on the occasion of JDF's twenty-fifth anniversary, we took stock of our progress and frustrations. We recognized that even with all the basic science progress that had been made, there was a major gap that was not going to be filled by anyone other than us—the need to focus much greater resources and efforts on moving scientific advances from the laboratory bench to the bedsides of our loved ones with diabetes.

So we redoubled our own fund-raising efforts, hired our first professional research staff, developed a road map of how research could get us to our cure goals, and launched a very aggressive government-relations program. The results have been extraordinary—we've awarded more than $1.3 billion to diabetes research, including hundreds of millions of dollars for stem cell research; and made significant breakthroughs in type 1 genetics, drug discovery, device development, and clinical trials. There have also been important discoveries that show real promise in the areas of islet replacement, beta cell regeneration, a closed-loop artificial pancreas development, prevention and treatment of complications, and prevention of type 1 in the first place.

These are accomplishments that naysayers repeatedly warned us could not be done (but we didn't listen). More important, these real accomplishments (gifts JDRF has given me and everyone with type 1) were the necessary stage-setters for what must come next.

And what is "next"? In the next five years, we will be raising the dollars necessary to fund $1 billion for cure-related therapeutics.

To celebrate my twenty-three years of service as international chairman of the Juvenile Diabetes Research Foundation, in November 2007, at a formal ball, I accepted a check for research funding in the amount of $23 million to launch the Forever Moore Initiative. I am told it will further attract more money for research.

Contributions have come from chapters everywhere, with gracious nods from businesses, individuals, and corporations to encourage the furtherance of "Bench to Bedside" science. I'm tired of curing diabetes in mice. We need to see more relevant statistics from and for humans. The mice will have to wait. It's long been a prayer of mine to reduce animal work and move on to human experimentation.

It's difficult to express my awe at receiving this enormous honor. To this day, I'm slightly surprised when I'm recognized in public and a kind word regarding my work is made. It's always lovely to hear but causes me to question, just a little, the qualifications of my admirer.

So, to be acknowledged at this level is as difficult to grasp as is the image of my father with a grin of pride on his face. But, you know what? In my second go-round at growing up, I'm learning that I can love this man and forgive him for being less than perfect. Though our roads have taken us to very different places, I can see similar strengths that have guided us: duty, loyalty, compassion—all standards that have made me a good person.

So I dedicate this honor to you, Dad, in the hope that it makes you smile as you say, "Well done, chum."

13

Searching and Researching

Science is hard to understand and accept sometimes. I grapple with it in some areas. And I have clear ideas about it when it comes to furthering the search for a cure.

I do understand that embryonic stem cell research raises concerns among people of goodwill, each trying to do what is right based on their very personal religious and moral beliefs. I have not shied from that personal soul-searching, nor has JDRF in its policy making, nor should anyone. I have found comfort in my heartfelt view that human stem cell research is truly life affirming. It is a direct outcome of a young family making a choice, without coercion or compensation, to donate for research an in vitro fertilized egg that was never implanted in a woman. It's an egg that otherwise would have been discarded or frozen forever. Because of the great potential of stem cell research, donating unused fertilized eggs is much like the life-giving choice a mother whose child has died tragically in an automobile accident makes when donating her child's organs to save another mother's child. It is the true pinnacle of charity to give so totally, so freely of oneself, to give life to another. Public support for stem cell research is an extension of this affirmation of life and is the best way to ensure that it is undertaken with the highest ethical standards. It offers hope for each of us, and that hope is not measured by numbers. It is ultimately personal. New therapies derived from embryonic stem cell research, conducted with public support by scientists from all areas of the globe, and made available to all who might benefit, are part of our broader vision of better health for all.

Since we're getting into areas about which I feel passionate but know I'm not a medical expert, I'd like to bring in one of the world's leading experts on stem cells, Douglas Melton, Ph.D. He has two children with type 1 diabetes and he is urgently leading the quest for ways to cure the disease. Doug is the Thomas Dudley Cabot Professor in the Natural Sciences at Harvard, an investigator at the Howard Hughes Medical Institute, and codirector of the Harvard Stem Cell Institute.

Q: *What is it about stem cells that offers one of the greatest hopes to finding a cure to type 1?*

DM: One of the unusual features of type 1 diabetes is that there is only one cell missing, the cell called the beta cell, which makes insulin. This presents a relatively simple problem, on the face of it: how to make more beta cells. The way scientists think about that problem now is that there are maybe two ways to replace the beta cells. One requires knowing a bit about how beta cells are replaced in our body. And all experiments in animals show that a beta cell is replaced by the division of a preexisting beta cell—a beta cell divides and makes two copies of itself.

And in normal people it is how our body replenishes the beta cells, not from stem cells. This is in contrast to the blood, for example, in which stem cells make more blood. But when a person has type 1 and beta cells are destroyed, there are no beta cells to replace those that die off . . . or at least not enough.

Q: *What does it have to do with stem cells?*

DM: Nothing yet. Given that there are too few beta cells in the patient and too few cadavers to provide beta cells for study, we are at a loss to get enough. You can use pig islets . . . but then you have another rejection problem.

Perhaps a better solution would be if you could make ones that come from your own body—suck out some beta cells and have them replicate and then reintroduce them in sufficient numbers into the body. That would be good. But the pancreas is a very unusual organ in that the beta cells are like tiny little seeds peppered throughout it, and all around them are important other cells that secrete all the enzymes you have ever heard of into your intestines— so if you go in and mess around in the pancreas you cause a lot of trouble.

So the excitement of stem cells is simply that they are another source of beta cells. Stem cells grow like weeds and divide very easily. Beta cells don't grow very much. The problem is that when a stem cell starts to differentiate, it wants to make all kinds of tissue—we need to fully understand what makes each stem cell make the choice to be a beta cell or not. That's what we study; that's what we are working on.

Q: *So why are embryonic stem cells superior to work with?*

DM: ESCs are superior to every other kind of stem cell you can use because they have more flexibility and options in the way they can be manipulated. ESCs can make pancreatic beta cells, and we'd like to harness that potential and make beta cells for transplantation into patients.

Q: *Have you established new ESC lines?*

DM: Yes, more than anywhere else.

Q: *The federal government had existing stem cell lines, and those you can get federal financing for. So what's wrong with the old ones, and why do you need new ones to do your work?*

DM: The government really only had four or five functional lines, and they were already known to be deficient in some ways. Stem cells grow forever and people think once you have them in a dish they will divide and grow forever. But after a certain number of passages they lose some of their potential.

I also knew we would need more lines because if you

take all mouse ESC lines and compare them they are al-most virtually identical—because they are inbred. But the human population is not inbred and only two of the human ESC lines are really good at making pancreatic beta cells, so we need to make new ones.

14

Pump It Up?

Okay. I own my diabetes. I talk about it before Congress. I am not hiding from the follies that my emerging disabilities subject me to—think Travolta—but some things are harder to accept than others, and for me the insulin pump has been, was, a big bump in the road. Let me explain.

Body image is important. It contributes to how you see yourself in your mind's eye—your inner reflection of your outward appearance to the world. Involving oneself in athletic activities—walking at a good pace, dancing, team sports—is especially important for good health and steady diabetes management. You want to like yourself and also set goals and aspirations for a healthy, attractive self. You want always to try becoming a little more physically fit. And you want to get to a place where your body gives you strength and confidence as a result.

That's what dance has given me—a sense of power and ownership of my body. But that positive image isn't just a result of dance; it is also something that I inherited, I think. And like all things familial, it comes with the good and the bad.

An example, you say? When it came time in the not-so-distant past to consider going on an insulin pump, I came face-to-face with my self-image—and that made it all a little tricky.

My family, for as long as I've been with them, has chosen to be tall and slim, possessing great posture. Father, six foot three; mother, five foot eight; her sisters used nines and tens as the inch markers; my brother, John, was six foot eight. At five feet seven and a quarter inches, I'm the runt. The reason for citing these measurements is for background. The body's poetry is something I've always respected. The idea of putting a tube into my body from the pump with its semipermanent plastic box riding along wherever I go, whatever I do—well, I'm ashamed of myself for being a little neurotic—I just hated the idea. I consoled myself by thinking that the reason women resist the pump more than men do is because men already have something attached to them. Forgive me for that.

But I am capable of giving myself a stern talking to—and that's what I did over and over until I was determined to fight through my fear of the pump and triumph as, well, sort of Mary d'Arc. Eventually, the idiocy in my thinking became obvious to me. Here I was putting off a step that might save my life because of mental obstacles that could be overcome with a bit of the old spunk of yore. Well, "spunk" might be out of the question, but surely "can do" is within the realm of possibility.

Once I uncovered my own particularly stubborn resistance to the pump, it made me realize that when my dad was facing his own version of this body-image issue, none of my neuroses or fears prevented me from dishing out advice on how to manage difficult medical situations. In the final ten years of his life, my father, not so happily, wore a colostomy bag—the result of benign yet complicated colon surgery. I remember talk-ing to him in a professorial tone about the functions of the body, its mysteries, stressing the advances in science and the miracles that were allowing us our lives. His was a far more in-vasive and complicated situation than mine to deal with, but in time, he came to accept it (the changing of the bag, etc.) and began treating it all as he did the bother of shaving or wa-tering the lawn, trips to the dentist—nuisances that must be endured—and I was, no doubt, one of them.

But, despite my pomposity, I was able to use my experience with diabetes to encourage my father to think positively, to be able to cope with feelings that take you to the edge of despair and then fly over that chasm to, well—less despair.

Robert plays that role with me—not the pompous part—the part where he helps me fly over that chasm of despair to Hawaii. But there are some things about Mary that even he, with his wis-dom and stubbornness in equal measure, cannot change, such as her inability to deal with electronics of any sort. Notice my sud-den use of the third person here. It just came out that way and I think it's because I'm a bit embarrassed by my failure. It was once cute—not anymore.

For example, I am unable to control the temperature in my own house! Robert, who is truly gifted with computers, cal-culators, and such, chose a state-of-the-art heating and air-conditioning system that we fight about and cheat over. (I know a couple of elves who are willing to come to my aid when icicles form on various body parts). This masterful piece of electronic gadgetry presents itself on a plasma screen that uti-lizes changeable grids for each room, with current readings appearing when you touch the screen in a specified order. If you make a mistake during the sequence, it all returns to the start! And you trudge onward once more, shivering uncontrollably. All right, I exaggerate. But a scientist I simply ain't—I appreciate the beauty of the arc of a missile's trajectory, but that's as far as the connection goes.

Many years ago, out of curiosity and boredom during the middle of a three-month hiatus from *The MTM Show,* I took an aptitude test to see what possible purpose I might have served had performing not chosen me. It was a thorough three-hour session delving into my strengths and weaknesses both emotional and intellectual, the outcome of which showed that while I have an average IQ, I function at a fourth-grade level in math! This was a shock, especially while learning that my low level of performance in math actually has a name. It was—is—called dyscalculia (the mathematical equivalent of dyslexia). Dyslexics have trouble processing words while dyscalculians—ics?—have trouble balancing a checkbook, overtip outrageously and for the wrong reason, and must absent themselves from the card game 21 (unable to add quickly and accurately enough). Oddly, I'm pretty good at geometry, which has helped me enormously in life. I'm anxiously waiting to see how!

Perhaps you're eager, or mildly interested, in learning which career was found to be most suitable for me. The top choice—modeling. Next, becoming a member of the armed forces.

I'm sure my fight with electronics is informed by the trouble I have with mathematics—and that it has played a big role in my difficulty accepting the pump. But maybe, just maybe, there's another side to my reticence about it. Not that I came up with this concept on my own, and not that I was entirely convinced, but according to Dr. Levy, I just might have been

getting in my own way by being too tough on myself. (Me?) I'd
set myself up for disappointment just when I needed a jolt of
invincibility. She had given me one instruction: "If you want to
go on the pump, you must be able to pay careful attention to
blood glucose levels day in and day out." She also insisted that
I pay consistent attention to carbohydrates, activity, and stress.
Those tasks were not at the time, nor are they now (I must confess), anything with which I have much luck.

What I heard was that, after all my agonizing internal de-
bating about the pump, I was deemed unworthy, "not quite
up to it!"

So I started keeping a daily chart (as I did when first diagnosed some thirty-eight years ago) consisting of the time of
blood tests and their results before breakfast, lunch, dinner,
and bedtime. Two hours after meals, I tested again and would
select the amount of bolus insulin that might be needed. I
also entered what I ate, how much of it, and the carbohydrate
count.

Dr. Levy suggested (of all the nerve!) that I might employ a
little more discretion when facing the dessert choices. You see, I
wrestle with an addiction to mocha cake. I'm often the loser in
the struggle to correct the glucose damage with that extra dose of
insulin. But of course it upsets the continuity of control. *Foiled!*

So as this old dog tried to teach herself the new trick, I
also started looking into which pump would work best for me
given my particular ineptitudes. I did want to succeed, so I
needed to select one that had the lowest possible opportunity
for mistakes—"child friendly."

But we thought that before we did the pump, why not try
one of these new continuous glucose monitors (CGM) that

everyone at JDRF was raving about. That and a pump make for a ultra-effective way to guard against highs and lows and to maintain steady control. And Dr. Levy wanted me to have less dramatic swings in my glucose levels—my lows are well-documented, and my highs, well, I do tiptoe up to 400 on a really bad day. My A1Cs? Not the recommended 7, I can tell you that. Sometimes even more than 9. So the folks from one of the CGM manufacturers sent a couple of wonderful people and a model for me to try.

"The truth is that right off the bat it was clear that Mary was never going to calibrate the device or keep tabs on or even be able to read the results easily," says Robert.

Did I ask for the truth? How did you get in here? Oh, I guess I'll take it easy—it's just hard for me to admit to all this. Anyway, when my ineptitude became clear, that's when Robert stepped up and volunteered to try the CGM on himself for a few days. That way he would really understand it and he could be better prepared to help me learn the ins and outs of the mechanism.

"I had my share of trouble with it," says Robert. "A few of the sensor pads were damaged—user error, I am sure. And it clearly gave different readings than the regular glucose monitor that I was also using for comparison purposes. But the technology is vastly improved from those first models, and the work being done to perfect them and make them work with the insulin pump is truly exciting. It promises to offer a great leap forward in control, and in improving the quality of life for people with diabetes." (For more information on the continuous glucose monitor and the artificial pancreas, see the Appendix, page 186.)

So, no CGM for me. No improved glucose control. No technology savvy. No pump. But that's me.

I think one has to assess the self pretty thoroughly to determine the likelihood of success with these promising contributions to control. And given my inclinations, fears, way of living, age, and general shortcomings, I must decline the opportunity science has given me. This may not be necessary for all patients, but the final decision-making factor for me is in the added revelation that I would be expected to set the alarm for three A.M. to do another blood test.

Nothing is final, though, so keep me in your thoughts.

All this pumping made me think about checking in again with the "kids who know everything." I was curious to find out who used a pump and what they thought about it. Allison, one of the kids who spent the afternoon with me at JDRF, told me she has had the pump since she was eleven years old. "The pump was easier for me because I had some pretty good motivation. I was embarrassed to give myself a shot in a restaurant, and I really like the pump for that. Plus, my parents noticed that after I got the pump my grades improved. I think it was because I got a lot better control of my blood sugar. When your sugar is high or low, it's harder to concentrate. And when I got my 'new best friend,' things got easier and clearer."

But the kids didn't all have the same point of view: Samantha joined in, saying, "I was on one pump, but there were issues with it, so I stopped using it. I'm a senior in high school and I'm going to college next year. I want to go on another pump before that because I will be on a completely different schedule, and I think it will be easier."

Will Smith, twenty, more man than boy, doesn't use a pump either. He was diagnosed ten years ago and has participated in several JDRF programs. "I was on the pump during my sophomore year in high school and I didn't like it," he says. "I was lackadaisical about changing the site and I had to disconnect it all the time because I was playing two sports. My doctor is always suggesting that I go back on it, but I am still on syringes and really happy with that system. It's like, if it isn't broken, why fix it? I don't know, maybe I'll consider it later in life. But it is pretty easy right now."

Maybe I am not so out of it, after all. The pump is a wonderful tool, but it's not for everyone—yet. As science continues its detective work in the lab, a small miracle may evolve and the continuous glucose monitor and the insulin pump will become one. Then we will have, thanks in large part to the funding support from JDRF, an artificial pancreas. And that's some pretty fancy footwork.

•   •   •

A valuable help from my physician has been the use of a chart for calculating the impact of what I eat, the amount of insulin I take, and the exercise I do, and tracking the hour of each event. The primary use of this method is to let you and your M.D. see and remember the trends resulting from your daily routine.

I e-mail my weekly test results to her, and when she spots an irregularity she calls me with suggestions for improvement and, if I need it, a pep talk. Your doctor may have his or her own chart. Do try it.

Blood Glucose Monitoring/Food Diary

Date: __ / __ / __

Patient Name: _____

	12 A.M.	1 A.M.	2 A.M.	3 A.M.	4 A.M.	5 A.M.	6 A.M.	7 A.M.	8 A.M.	9 A.M.	10 A.M.	11 A.M.	12 P.M.	1 P.M.	2 P.M.	3 P.M.	4 P.M.	5 P.M.	6 P.M.	7 P.M.	8 P.M.	9 P.M.	10 P.M.	11 P.M.
Blood Glucose																								
Carbohydrates																								
Meal Bolus																								
Correction Bolus																								
Basal Rate																								
Exercise																								
Urine Ketones																								
Set Change																								

Breakfast

Time	Food	Amount
8:00		

Morning Snack

Lunch

Time	Food	Amount

Afternoon Snack

Dinner

Time	Food	Amount

Evening Snack

Comments: _____

15

The Dance Goes On

Becoming chairman of JDRF changed my life and my relationship to diabetes dramatically. It punctuated my days with a chance to meet some of the sharpest scientific and medical minds. I've talked with hundreds of families and children who have shared their stories of contending with our common disease. It may seem ironic (I guess it does to me) that becoming chairman didn't do much to enlighten my own somewhat contentious relationship with the disease.

In fact, I have to acknowledge that over the years diabetes has proved resistant to my most fervent wish—that it not interfere with my life. And today, while I am finally smarter, less rigid, more willing to comply, I am also forced to deal with the repercussions of a life spent paying less attention to glucose control than I could have.

There are the frequent lows, the exhaustion that hits when I have gone too high (250 is not a stranger), the problems with my eyesight (although I can spot a misplaced comma at 100 yards), and my inability to walk much distance, as claudication makes it too painful.

I'm here to make myself an object lesson, if you will, and

to share with you a bit of wisdom from my doctor, who has helped me feel positive and more in control than ever: "Every small step I take is a victory," Dr. Levy says, "and every improvement is an important one. It's progress."

Those are the encouraging and very true words that she hurls at me whenever I see her. So for now, at least, I won't beat myself up about the past. They (whoever they are) always say it takes a team to establish good diabetes management. That's true. It takes a team to do almost anything worthwhile. That's a lesson I learned early on from the wonderful Carl Reiner. During the days of *The Dick Van Dyke Show,* whenever a cast member or one of the crew or a passing vagabond had a suggestion for a scene, Carl would take the proffered advice very seriously. "Listen," he'd say, "if it's a good suggestion, I take it and use it. I don't care if the craft service man, much less an actor, proffers it." That expansive, generous, and open-minded approach has stayed with me and influenced not only my work, but my personal life as well. The lessons one can learn in and from a group are so important.

Dr. Levy has a nurse educator and nutritionist who are integral parts of her team. As I've said repeatedly and can't say enough, she has helped me enormously to make more progress and fewer mistakes.

But I can't resist telling you about a couple of incidents. This is my favorite "low": Probably five or six summers ago, Robert and I joined our good friends Bernadette Peters and her husband, Michael Wittenberg (who so tragically died in 2005 in a helicopter crash), for a weekend at their summer rental in one of the Hamptons. I think it was East—no, perhaps

Northampton, because it took so long to get there. Wait—does a Northampton even exist? If not—why not? It could have been East. The house, a properly windblown, sand-on-the-porch kind of cottage, made you want to fast-forward to a slight sunburn under the white cotton shift (the one you forgot to pack), happily shucking clams.

As instructed, I wore exercise garb so we could head straight to the gym before lunch. Bernadette drove us, while Robert and Michael opted to run there.

Our adventure started out badly. As Bernadette tried to extricate her new Hummer from an impossible parking spot between two rather docile-looking vehicles, I popped my head out the passenger window which her directions to guide her through the back-and-forthing to come. My reportage was soon interrupted by the window, which was suddenly rising threateningly toward my neck, which, of course, was attached to my head on the outside of the car! Apparently this wasn't the tolerant kind of window that stops once it sees what it's doing.

Bernadette and I were both shrieking now. Well, one was shrieking. The other, me, was glunting and werging as Bernadette fumbled for the up/down button.

Even though all of the above took no more than three seconds, it felt as though my "near-death scene" would cause this "film" to run too long (the result of a good deal of overacting on my part). Suddenly the window ceased its death stalk and I could retrieve my head safely into the car. We looked at each other solemnly and then burst into uncontrollable laughter— just face-to-face hysteria.

After catching our breath and reliving the step-by-step

actions that caused "the little horror," we made our way to the gym.

Bernadette was eager for me to work out with the coach she liked so much. After our introduction she went off to her tennis lesson, still giggling and looking over her shoulder at me. I made my way to the running track with Nord, an Icelandic husky trainer (he was husky, too) in his midtwenties.

There was something about him that made me pay attention. He spoke quickly at a low volume with what must have been an Icelandic accent. And he rarely smiled, even though he was on vacation. I was determined to keep up with everything he showed me, including the brisk trot that he set as our pace to the track. But, hallelujah! We were in the country!—forest, hillsides, huge rocks and their offspring, the pebbles that were tripping me up as I struggled to keep in stride with the Viking.

We finally reached the track and circled at a faster pace than I'd expected. I was happy at last, upon completion, only to then be cast to the ground for push-ups, so many that my biceps and tris were shaking. I heard him utter a snicker kind of snort—empathy? I don't think so.

Before long I was plunged into a series of lunges and jumps. Could it have been both at the same time? Maybe. It was brutal, but I needed to triumph here to impress him with something, even if it was simply my determination to do more than he thought I could.

After an hour or so, we called it a day and headed back to the gym, me stumbling faithfully behind my tormentor. On the way, a familiar weakness tapped me on the shoulder and I felt my competitive alter ego diminish a bit. I hated to do it, but I had no choice, so I confessed that I had overdone it and needed to get some orange juice soon. The bigger part of the problem was that I didn't know if I could make it back to the gym without further lowering the glucose in my system. Here's where some algebra would have come in handy: Get there fast, covering a distance of X in Y minutes, and factoring in the glucose level of Z. If this data were available, one would probably divide the sum of some of that information after multiplying it by another equation.

Look, Nord, I have diabetes and I'm afraid I shouldn't have been, uh . . .

"Showing off?" he offered. "Lady, you definitely have spunk!" But he smiled and said, "We'll get you there."

And with that he hoisted me over his shoulder. Being slung over a shoulder always looks to be carefree, but it's tough on the belly, let me tell you! En route, it became clear that conversation was out of the question, at least for me. So with nothing else to do, I began noticing things. I noticed that I'd been using my left hand's fingertips more than the right in checking my blood, since there was more callusing on those lefties than there should be. (There are now devices that give more options for testing than just the fingers. See the Appendix, page 170.) I also saw plenty of mushrooms camping at the base of trees. Surely there is some easy way to identify the edible mushrooms from the masqueraders waiting to poison you. Plus, I found that a man's rear loses all its appeal when viewed upside down. Now why should that be? Finally, my thoughts went to how forever grateful to this hero I'd be.

By the time Nord had stopped and set me to the task of walking up the steps of the center, Robert and Michael had returned, as well.

"Blood sugar," Nord said to a startled Robert as I wove my way toward him.

"A pretty severe one, too," Robert observed. "Where are those vending machines?" he demanded of Michael. And around the corner they rushed, leaving me where I sat and, according to Bernadette, studied Nord's rear with great concentration.

Within seconds, my Lone Ranger and Tonto soared back into the room, arms loaded with all sorts of juices, candy, and cakes. I grabbed a bottle of red stuff and downed it fast as I could, and then spotted an intriguing package of what looked to be two small chocolate cakes wrapped around a cream filling. Michael said, "Mary, you'll love these and they're so sugary!"

When you've turned your back on junk like that for so long, and you find yourself in the throes of hypoglycemia, it's your fantasy come true. Now, one thinks, I can eat this! Not only that, I should and must eat it! I've earned this and I can enjoy it! Well, that's what I thought. I ate 'em, but I don't do that now. There are safer treats you should ask your doctor about.

Ready for another episode in Mary's Follies? This time it takes place on a national stage. In May 2008, Oprah asked the cast of *The Mary Tyler Moore Show* to join her for an hour of reverie, heartfelt hugging, and, hopefully, laughter. What a treat to float in all the above!

In order to speak coherently with the "O" woman, I ran some tales of yore through my head, but it was difficult to recall one that hadn't already had its moment in the sun.

A bit of a refresher course in the Juvenile Diabetes Research Foundation's stats—research updates, breakthroughs in the

science of living with the disease, monies raised to date, etc.—
and I was free to make appointments for a manicure and hair
color touchup. God forbid I'd look my age!

As I'm plowing through the cobwebs of memory for humorous anecdotes to have ready, I remembered the time the
show had returned from our spring hiatus, looking forward to
settling into our new dressing rooms—all redecorated and
moved around a bit to accommodate those of us who needed
to be closer to the set for the many changes of wardrobe required.

Well, here comes the story: I pushed through the heavy
soundproof door of our home, Stage 2, and despite the dim
lighting strolled to what I thought was my dressing room. I
opened the door just in time to lock eyes with a glistening Ed
Asner as he stepped out of the shower! As he made a mad dash
for a towel that wasn't there, I, too, quickly backed out of the
room, knocking over a misplaced standing lamp en route.

Ed and I have never spoken of that brief encounter. It's the
kind of occurrence that needs to be faced right away or not at
all, don't you think? I do feel obliged to remark that the rave
reviews of his enormous talent through the years should not
be limited to what you see on screen.

So I didn't share that story with Oprah. You're getting it
firsthand now.

I think my sugar is low.

Back now. I was right—55. Not awful, but unsettling just
the same. I'm aware of the approaching "dips" even when I'm at
65. And that gives me an alarm to check it out and grab something sweet.

Now, back to Oprah. I'll never forget the impact of the sets they built for our visit and the attention to details of each—the newsroom at WJM, complete with a rose on my desk and typewriters for all! (Where did they find them—even one?) Mary's living room, looked over by the ceramic pumpkin-shaped cookie jar, gave me a rather painful throat clutch. That boastful letter "M" held forth on the wall near the front door, and every piece of furniture mirrored the original.

Among my favorite playthings growing up was a dollhouse that called to me long after it was age appropriate. I've often thought that the many houses and apartments I've lived in as I blithely moved from one to the other might be the result of my still longing to redecorate that magical little house.

It strikes me as odd that I never noticed the absence of hallways or that there was no back of the dollhouse at all! Every film set consists of the same three-wall configuration—maybe that's why I've always felt comfortable on a set.

It was an uneasy feeling wanting to talk with "Madame O" but at the same time being drawn into all the corners of that living room, reliving the many moments with Valerie, Cloris, Betty, and Georgia through seven years that cracked like a whip—over too soon.

The set that was the WJM newsroom was just as meticulously brought to life as my beloved apartment had been. Oprah had decided to open the show with her sitting at my desk in the empty newsroom as I did my best impersonation of Ted Baxter pompously swinging his body through those double doors to announce his entrance with a basso profoundo "Hi, guys!" I'm told there's hardly an office in America that doesn't have its own Ted attempting that entrance.

Well, as Oprah sat at my single-rose-adorned desk, sharing

memories with her audience, I was to offer my version of Ted's moment by trumpeting, "Hi, Oprah," all to be followed by the host/celebrity embracing at center stage.

There was just one problem to be overcome. While giving the preshow tour of these new sets, the assistant director pointed out a slight deviation from the original, and the difference was in the floor level. Unlike with the old set, upon entering through the new set's two doors there was a drop of about ten inches. The young man apologized for it, explaining that it was an accommodation for pipes that couldn't be moved. I was so grateful to him for warning me about it. With my vision problems, imagine what small disaster could befall your most earnest Mary.

After a few more powder puffings and such, it was, "Places, please," and there sat "Miss O" at my old desk, talking to her audience about our show and how it had touched her.

Peeking between the split of those doors, I was fascinated to see how rapt those women were. And while I'm peeking, I thought, let's check out the step-down about two feet away. Oprah was effusive in her words of introduction to me, so much so that as I heard my name, excitement propelled me through the doors and toward her without the necessary adjustment (like bending my knees) needed to make the step, the step I had just pointed out to myself. I flew for a bit, bent forward, my feet making futile attempts to find the ground. My arms, I remember, were also searching for some assistance. And suddenly there she was! Walking toward me with a warm smile on her Oprah Winfrey face to clutch me. We continued into the not-unexpected air-kissing of host and actress, but this time, I promise you, it was heartfelt.

Since this particular episode had been taped, I hoped that my stumble would be cut out in that magical way that tape editors can save lives and reputations. But then I thought, no, it's an opportunity to be real and show that I can be and often am a rival to Dick Van Dyke, who's famous for his pratfalls.

Turns out all of us had so much fun recollecting and laughing that the show ran fourteen minutes over, so they were grateful for every cut they could make.

Well, all right, I guess I can live with my perfection.

16

It's a Jungle Out There

Last July, I was awakened from my suburban doldrums when I was asked to play Brooke Shields's mother in two episodes of her series, *Lipstick Jungle*. It was so renewing to be wanted again for the ability just below the surface of this comfortable Connecticut wife, mother of four dogs, best friend to some, chairman of JDRF, and builder of a new house, who was pining once again to hear laughter from an audience. Or to simply stand next to the one who does.

Joyce (my character) is a hard-nosed businesswoman who, after enjoying many successful years as chief operating officer of a large corporation, has retired and is finding it difficult to fill her now empty life. "I've run out of cruises, I'm done re-upholstering, and I can't find anyone who'll have dinner with me later than four-thirty!" She's been a loving, if controlling, figure in Wendy's (Brooke's) life and descends on her and her family in hopes of renewing her reign as master of all she surveys.

Wendy is wrestling with the maternal guilt that most working mothers feel and is now drowning in her own mother's counsel against jeopardizing her flourishing career as a studio chief.

I loved the story line and couldn't wait to begin work. Threatening this enticing opportunity, however, was the ill-timed accident I'd had three weeks or so before.

One afternoon while I was crossing the kitchen from table to sink with an "eaten clean" cake plate in hand, my miniature schnauzer, Shana, took that opportunity to investigate my actions and quickly dashed before me on her way to where the "goods" were headed. Due to my lack of peripheral vision, I, of course, didn't see her self-serving move and tripped over her. I didn't just trip—I took flight really, and then made a perfect one-point landing on my left knee.

As I was told by friends who have suffered broken bones, there is no pain at first, just confusion as to why the earth is ending its life at this time. There'd been no whispers about its probability, and the sun was shining, so how could it? And then—oh my God! The stabbing, red-hot dagger that cleaved my tiny kneecap engulfed me! They tell me in my delirium I scrabbled around the floor, dripping tears and, despite the pain, looking for icing-smeared shards of the broken plate beneath and around me (I am relentlessly neat and tidy). The accident was, no doubt, punishment for the irresponsible eating of that cake. But it was mocha!

I'm still unable to recall it, but Robert, who was home at the time, and Terry managed to wedge me into the car amid howling protests at the added discomfort and got me to the emergency room before I died.

The diagnosis: a fractured patella (kneecap), which was immediately immobilized in an unbending soft cast.

If you live in a two-story house and must use the stairs, the only way to accomplish this without bending the injured knee is to ascend by raising the good knee while the injured one remains straight and repeat and repeat and repeat. For descending, keep the injured knee straight and step down with it. Try remembering the (up-to-this-point-useless) adage "Up with the good, down with the bad." Or run like hell singing "We Shall Overcome."

With the isolated inaction of the knee for at least seven weeks, I couldn't imagine how the show would accommodate my infirmity in front of the camera. "Don't worry," I was told. "When we shot the pilot last year, Brooke was recuperating from a broken foot. So we learned lots of tricks to hide it. Will your trousers fit over the brace?"

"I'll see to it," I said, and off to Armani I limped.

The filming experience was creatively rewarding and fun. Brooke is a great sparring partner and the director, Timothy Busfield, equaled the inspiration and strength of Jay Sandrich, who directed almost all of the *MTM Show* episodes. He also developed new and intriguing approaches to the kinds of interactions on which I'd cut these veteran teeth!

A part of my business, ever unchanging, is what we always referred to as the photographers (aka the paparazzi) that crop up just when you've forgotten how intrusive they can be.

On our first day of filming, we were having a good time shopping for fruit in the outdoor market of Tompkins Square Park when a seemingly harmless group of ten or so smiling, waving men bearing cameras descended upon us. They were quite respectful of our needed space and seemed not to mind being cautioned. So all went well.

The next day, the company moved inside the converted warehouse that served as our studio, and I enjoyed four days of palling around with Brooke and Co.

The next week I shrieked as I came upon the front-page coverage of that day in the park. It was one of those stupid glossies that you buy in grocery stores and the like. There were pictures of me out of costume in walking shorts, which we were all wearing because of the heat. I didn't think that in revealing my cast it would so absurdly be used to create an untrue exposé. The headline shouted that I was "facing an amputation." And as if that weren't enough, I was also "nearly blind" and "living with a brain tumor." The creative madman chose to say in closing that my "other leg didn't look so good, either!"

Also untrue. It's quite comely.

I don't think I'll file suit for a retraction. One rarely triumphs in facing their army of liars, but my accompanying protest would be on behalf of the family members and friends who believed it. It did cause some distress. So much for my friendly waves to the paparazzi! From now on, they'll be met with scowls, which will, of course, be met with a follow-up story on my tragic stroke.

Much to my pleasure, I've just been given the start date for episode two, and without even reading the script, my pulse has quickened.

Clearly, I have enough adventures without all the added fantasies that float through the tabloids. Case in point: Shortly after the filming was over I found myself once again in Dr. Levy's office telling her about my most recent low. It had happened just a little while before. Would you believe I injected the wrong insulin? Well, I did! For years, I have taken two very different types of insulin every day. One, in a short bottle, is used before each meal, therefore fast-acting. It's called NovoLog. The other I take before bed to cover my blood sugar chemistry slowly during the night. It's called Lantus. It lives in a taller, skinny bottle, and I do know the difference. On this particular night, without thinking, I filled my syringe with ten units of what should have been the long-acting insulin, but instead gave myself ten units of the fast-acting, heavy-duty insulin that should have been followed by a full meal. It wasn't.

Robert had been called to JDRF Research Committee and board meetings in downtown Manhattan that evening. At eleven P.M. I woke up to hear pounding on the doors, first the front door and then the kitchen one, accompanied by the muffled yet distinctive voice of Robert saying something about a key. I got up—and when I say I got up, I mean I awoke fully—and yet I was not fully alert. And so I just sat on my bed, crossly awaiting Robert's explanation for the pounding and yelling.

He was surprised that I hadn't come down to the kitchen to see what the racket was all about. I was later to find out that the problem was caused by two coincidental missteps. One was our loving housekeeper's automatically locking the door as she does if Robert is not home, expecting him to use his key. On this night, however, he forgot to take it with him, placing a snirch of guilt upon his shoulders.

According to Robert, through the window he saw Anya, the housekeeper, come flying down the stairs looking a little like Angela Lansbury piloting a goose—her blond hair flying and bathrobe tripping her as she ran.

Robert then came quickly upstairs, morbidly imagining the

worst. He says I was lying on my side in bed with one foot on the floor. I was staring straight ahead and made no move to acknowledge his presence. He lifted me up and carried me to the bathroom, where my blood-testing equipment is, and, with Anya's help, pricked my finger, produced some blood, and tested it on the meter. It was 30!—very, very low. We have five or six glucagon emergency kits stashed in various places in the house so that one is always handy. And so it was that the ultimate instrument—a prepared syringe of glucose—in counteracting a low was used to very good effect. It took about twenty minutes before I felt like a normal human being, during which time I perspired profusely, as always in these circumstances. When the schvitzing abated, I took a shower, mostly to warm me up because I was now (again, not unexpectedly) freezing. What a roller coaster!

I tell you all this because I want you to know (it took me many years to understand) that when dealing with a low, remember that the chaos will cease, your body will again function as it's supposed to, and your world will not have stopped turning if you're prepared to deal with it.

So what does this all mean in the slow reeducation, the growing up again of Mary Tyler Moore? That I'm never going to stop trying, and learning, and goofing up, apparently. And that in the great scheme of things, you always need a good support team—be it a husband and a doctor, a diabetes educator, and/or a relative or a friend. Don't ever try to manage this in isolation. Carl Reiner and *The Dick Van Dyke Show* certainly taught me at a young age, and it was reinforced by *The Mary Tyler Moore Show,* that an ensemble is more than the sum of its parts. What we created from the magic chemistry of us all working together, caring about one another's triumphs and bruises—that's a lesson in the power of "the team."

So I guess what I'm asking is, will you join the JDRF team? Will you let me join yours? Because together we can have a pretty good time and do a lot to make sure that future generations will never have to face the struggles to control their blood sugar that we have had to contend with.

We're going to make it after all.

Appendixes

A. Diabetes 101

If you have just been diagnosed (or are the loved one of someone who has), it can all seem overwhelming and hard to get a handle on. But kids master the pump; adults learn to understand all the complexities of how to adjust insulin and food intake; everyone becomes more expert than may seem imaginable to you right now. So to help you get started, here's a short course on the world of diabetes.

The Basics

Something called islet cells are scattered throughout the pancreas, a palm-size organ that sits behind the lower part of the stomach. They, in turn, are made up of several types of cells, including beta cells—and that's where insulin is produced.

Type 1 diabetes happens when the body launches an immune system attack on its own insulin-producing beta cells

Kalia Doner, research editor, is editor-in-chief of *Diabetes Focus* magazine, former publications manager of the Juvenile Diabetes Research Foundation, and author or co-author of more than twenty-five books, many on health and wellness.

in the pancreas. The result is that the beta cells are killed off in sufficient quantities to deprive the body of the hormone insulin. This matters because insulin is the key that opens the door of our body's cells. This makes it possible for energy (glucose) in our bloodstream to move into each of our body's cells, where it powers their every activity. When that cannot happen, the glucose remains in the bloodstream, blood sugar levels soar, and the cells are starved. But this does not (usually) happen quickly. Mark Atkinson, Ph.D., of the University of Florida's Departments of Pathology and of Pediatrics, explains: "Whatever it is that causes type 1, for most people these processes seem to start early—in the first fifteen to twenty-four months of life. And it can take years or decades for symptoms of type 1 to occur. In many settings when someone is diagnosed with type 1, they will ask 'Why me?' And the doc will say, 'Oh, you had a viral infection.' It is true that viruses could be involved with type 1, but not in the way most people, including physicians, think. A lot of textbooks told medical students twenty to thirty years ago that type 1 was triggered by a recent viral infection. But it's a fictional concept that's taken root and remains in the minds of many doctors today. We now know that diabetes doesn't develop that way. It takes months to decades for the immune response to develop the disease."

To confirm the slow progression of type 1 diabetes, JDRF has put together an incredibly innovative program that's looking at the validity of a couple of other long-held medical opinions about diabetes: that 80 to 90 percent of beta cells are destroyed by the time you are diagnosed with diabetes and that within a couple of years of diagnosis all the beta cells are killed off and you don't have any more at all. Dr. Atkinson explains: "Recently, researchers have discovered that for some people, symptoms of type 1 develop when only fifty percent or so of the islets are destroyed. Therefore it's likely variable from person to person and may depend on their age, physical activities, weight, and other factors. This is very important information for researchers trying to reverse type 1 diabetes in those who are recently diagnosed. Therapies may be developed that will allow the remaining insulin-producing cells to function normally. As for the notion that insulin-producing cells may be present many years after diagnosis, well, some but certainly not all people who have had diabetes for decades seem to still be trying to make insulin-producing cells. But it also appears that the immune system is doing the job we don't want it to do—killing the newly formed insulin-producing cells."

So, over time the beta cells are killed and elevated glucose levels become dangerously high. That's when diagnosis is made and from then on chronic high glucose levels and other changes in body chemistry (inflammation, for example) may trigger a whole roster of diabetes-related complications—heart disease, kidney problems, nerve damage, and diabetic eye disease (retinopathy) are the major disorders.

The Technical Stuff That Matters

To really understand type 1 diabetes—who gets it, how it can be predicted, and how it affects the body—you need to know a bit about the body's immune system and what happens in it when diabetes strikes. Now, even scientists who devote their lives to these matters don't know all they'd like about how it works—and what happens when it goes awry. So don't think it all has to be perfectly clear to you. But sometimes you have to look at complicated medical matters to understand simple and important facts like "If one of my children has type 1 will the others develop it, too?" Or, "How likely am I to get type 1 if my mother had it?" "What are the risk factors and do we have any control over them?"

So, we are going to look at two topics: the role of genes and of the environment in the development of type 1 diabetes, and the autoimmune disease process and what it means for predicting who will or won't get the disease.

The Role of Genes and Environment

The current scientific consensus is that type 1 diabetes is brought on by the combination of a genetic predisposition (turns out there are many genes that may play a role, singly or in combination) and environmental triggers, as well as other biochemical activities in the body that are yet to be fully identified. According to Stephen S. Rich, Ph.D., Professor of Public Health Sciences and Director of the Center for Public Health Genomics at the University of Virginia, genes contribute about 40 or 50 percent of the risk for type 1. "The prevalence in the general population of type 1 is about one-half of a percent," he explains. "But to a brother or sister of someone with type 1 the risk is about eight percent, and that's a fifteen- to sixteen-fold increase in probability."

But genes are not the whole story. Studies of identical twins clearly show that it is not enough to have a genetic predisposition—if one identical twin gets diabetes before the age of six, the other has around a 60 percent chance of also being diagnosed; if one twin is diagnosed after the age of twenty-five then the risk to the other twin falls to only around

6 percent. Not so identical in either case. So what are the so-called environmental causes that make the difference between one twin getting the disease and another not?

You build up risk by adding more and more genetic factors until you reach a threshold where you may become particularly vulnerable to environmental triggers. You may also reach the threshold with a less heavy genetic burden but a heavier environmental burden. Each adds its own load. The way to get the threshold can be very individual.

One genetic background might make you vulnerable to one or more environmental triggers while another genetic background might make completely distinct triggers the trouble-makers. But in both cases, the result may be type 1 diabetes.

That slippery equation may explain why every couple of years you hear that one thing or another is a cause, and then those theories are supplanted by some other cause: viruses, cereals, childhood vaccinations, dairy products. The list is "longer than your arm," says Dr. Atkinson. The truth is, we don't yet fully understand what causes type 1 because so many different triggers may be involved.

The Role of the Immune System and Antibodies
When the immune system wants to fight off a potentially harmful virus or bacterium, it summons up parts of its own army of warrior cells—antibodies—to kill off the invaders. This is a wonderful thing, but sometimes it goes awry. For reasons that no one is sure of (it could be that the immune system itself goes off the tracks or, in the case of type 1 diabetes, it could be that the insulin-producing beta cells in the pancreas become deformed in some way), the immune system sometimes

attacks cells that are supposed to be in our body, not outside invaders. This is what happens when the immune system kills off the beta cells in the pancreas. As we have said, it takes months or years for so many to be killed that a person cannot produce enough insulin to remain healthy, and type 1 is diagnosed. But before that, the immune system antibodies that are attacking the beta cells are circulating through the blood and can be identified with a simple blood test.

Predicting Who Is at Risk

Even if scientists aren't sure what triggers lead to type 1 diabetes, they are now confident—as confident as science can be—of how to identify the people who are most likely to develop type 1 diabetes. Dr. Atkinson is one of many who has devoted his life to clarifying the causes of the disease and identifying methods that might work to prevent or reverse diabetes. He says that there are blood tests that can look at genetic- and immune-system markers (those antibodies) as well as a metabolic test that allows doctors to determine the degree of a person's risk for developing diabetes. "We have tests that provide a three-way analysis for pinpointing who is most vulnerable. They let us identify genes that carry a risk and antibodies to islets that reveal the destructive immune response, and give us the ability to measure how the body secretes insulin in response to eating carbohydrates. These tests don't mean we can predict with one hundred percent certainty who's going to get type 1 diabetes nor the date on which it will occur, but we are confident that nearly everyone meeting specific conditions will eventually develop the disease. Not everyone has heard of these tests, nor are they provided in most doctors' offices—yet. Until we find a way to prevent type 1 with near certainty, most of these tests will be used only for research. Many of us want to see the situation change for the better."

B. Good News, Bad News

The Good News

People with type 1 diabetes are living much, much longer and much, much healthier lives. According to the National Institute of Diabetes and Digestive and Kidney Diseases, a recent study showed just how dramatic the improvements are: "Scientists examined the rates of premature death and complications twenty to thirty years after diagnosis with type 1 diabetes in western Pennsylvania. Mortality at twenty years after diagnosis was reduced by 84 percent for those diagnosed from 1975 to 1980, compared to those diagnosed from 1950 to 1959. The prognosis continues to improve, with kidney failure, diabetic nerve damage, and premature death all less likely to occur now than in the past, as research has led to continuous improvements in therapy." We are getting better and better at managing blood glucose levels—better meters, incredibly sophisticated pumps, more knowledge about the way to use food and exercise to promote long-term health. . . . All of that makes the prognosis for people with type 1 markedly improved.

The Bad News

There is a noticeable increase in the number of very young children diagnosed with type 1. Various studies have confirmed these trends: The incidence of type 1 is increasing in Finland,

England, Norway, Israel, Austria, and several other countries. Here in the United States it is also on the rise. For example, in Colorado between 1978 and 2004 the incidence of type 1 diabetes increased by 2.3 percent a year. Why? Researchers can only speculate, but some have suggested that increased genetic transmission alone cannot account for the numbers and that the environment must have a larger role.

Type 2

The incidence of type 2 diabetes—when the body cannot use insulin properly or produce enough of it—has increased dramatically. According to Professor Francine Kaufman, M.D., head of the Center for Diabetes, Endocrinology, and Metabolism at Children's Hospital in Los Angeles, writing in the journal *Clinical Diabetes* in 2002, "Type 2 diabetes has been described as a new epidemic in the American pediatric population that has been coincident with the overall 33 percent increase in diabetes incidence and prevalence seen during the past decade. In 1992, it was rare for most pediatric centers to have patients with type 2 diabetes. By 1994, type 2 diabetes accounted for up to 16 percent of new cases of pediatric diabetes in urban areas, and by 1999, it accounted for 8 to 45 percent of new cases depending on geographic location." It particularly targets the African American, Hispanic, Native American, and Asian populations and seems to be due to a combination of insulin resistance and beta cell failure.

And among these children, the risk of developing serious diabetes-related complications, heart disease, and other physical problems is alarming—striking earlier and more severely than has been seen before. Most children who develop type 2 dia-

betes have a family member with the disease; 45 to 80 percent
have a parent with type 2 diabetes, and 74 to 90 percent report
at least one affected first- or second-degree relative. But obesity
is the most significant risk factor.

C. Diabetic Drills

Getting organized—that is a huge effort in the beginning (or if
you are like me, in the middle, too!). But once you do, it really
makes the various tasks of managing diabetes so much less intrusive and easier to take care of. So I offer you these
suggestions—a bulleted list of Dr. Levy's advice—for what to
do every day, each time you see your doctor, and once a year.

The Daily Drill
- Keep a daily record of blood glucose readings.
- Follow your nutritional plan, paying special attention to
  your intake of carbohydrates and fats.
- Get at least thirty minutes of physical activity every day.
  Ask your health-care provider to advise you about the best
  kinds of exercise and activities for you.
- Take all medication as directed.
- Talk to your doctor about any problems or concerns you
  have about your regimen—for example, let the doctor
  know if it is too difficult to follow, if you are missing injections, or if your numbers are not improving.
- Check your feet every day for cuts, blisters, sores, hot spots,
  swelling, or redness. If you have any of these problems,
  contact your doctor for advice on what to do. Also check

your shoes to make sure they do not have rough areas on the inside and that they fit your feet comfortably.

- Brush and floss your teeth twice a day. People with diabetes have an increased risk of gum disease, and it appears that gum disease makes it harder to control glucose levels.

The Doctor Drill

At every visit:

- Show your record of glucose readings to the doctor.
- Make sure to tell the doctor if you have had any lows.
- Have your doctor check your weight and blood pressure and inspect your feet. (Take your shoes off before the doctor comes into the examining room—that way you both will remember to do it.)
- Talk about your exercise routine and level of physical activity.
- Talk about stress that may be affecting your glucose levels and how to reduce it.
- If you smoke, ask for assistance in quitting.

Once or Twice a Year

- Have an A1C test to evaluate your level of glucose control over the previous three- or four-month period. Some doctors recommend A1C tests every three months.
- Have a blood test to check cholesterol and other blood lipid levels.
- Have kidney function tests: a microalbumin test to check for protein in the urine and a blood test to check on creatinine levels. Unless you monitor your kidney function

regularly, chances are you won't get diagnosed until kidney problems have become quite advanced, since they often don't cause symptoms in the early stages. Prompt diagnosis can help you avoid the more serious repercussions: dialysis and transplant.

- Once a year see an ophthalmologist (that's an M.D.) who is experienced in handling diabetes-related eye problems. Have a dilated eye exam.
- See your dentist twice a year for a cleaning and a checkup.
- Get a flu shot—studies show people with diabetes are more likely to contract the flu and that it is more severe when they do.
- Get a pneumonia vaccine if you are sixty-five or older and have not had one for five years or more.

D. Know Your Numbers

Always talk with your doctor about the right target numbers for you; these are the basic guidelines offered by the National Institute of Diabetes and Digestive and Kidney Diseases (NIDDK).

Glucose Targets: For most people with diabetes, 90 to 130 before meals; less than 180 one to two hours after the start of a meal.

Blood Pressure: Blood pressure is written with two numbers separated by a slash. The first number should be below 130 and the second number should be below 80—that's 130/80. If you already have kidney disease, ask your doctor what numbers are best for you.

Blood Lipids

Total cholesterol	below 200
LDL cholesterol	below 100
HDL cholesterol	above 40 (men)
	above 50 (women)
Triglycerides	below 150

E. Testing, Testing

Your glucose monitor is your best friend—a companion that should never leave your side. Your doctor may suggest that you test your blood sugar before you eat, two hours after meals, at bedtime, perhaps at 3 A.M., and anytime you experience signs or symptoms. That means you are testing up to eight or more times a day—triathletes and marathoners may test more than twelve times a day when they are in the throes of training or competition. You should also test more often when you change medications, when you have unusual stress or illness, or in other unusual circumstances.

Those are the guidelines today—but it wasn't until the 1980s that self-monitoring became accepted by the diabetes world. Until then many people (experts included) thought that the monitoring should be done only in a doctor's office. But the push from people with type 1 was so strong that the "experts" had to accept the inevitable, and that in turn led to better and better machines to test blood glucose levels. Today, the latest meters offer real-time glucose readings and high/low alerts. There are monitors that don't require coding and ones that deal with over- or underdosing. There are even wireless meters that communicate with insulin pumps and with continuous glucose sensors. And tomorrow promises to combine these sophisticated continuous glucose monitors with automatic insulin pumps that work together to create a closed-loop "artificial pancreas." The no-coding feature is important, according to *The Journal of Diabetes Science and Technology,* because it helps prevent over- or underdosing with insulin that can happen when a person either incorrectly codes the monitor or skips that step entirely. The inaccurate test data that may result can lead to serious symptoms and potentially long-term health problems.

Choosing and Using the Right Meter

Each meter differs in the amount of blood needed for a test, the speed that it reads the glucose levels, the size of the unit, its ability to store test results and to communicate with your computer, the cost of the unit and of the test strips or sensors. You can also get meters that have special features for those with manual dexterity problems or vision deficits.

When you get a new meter, meet with a diabetes educator or other trained health care professional to learn the particular ins and outs of that meter. Always test a new meter's accuracy using a quality-control solution: you know the solution's glucose value before the test and can compare it with the meter's readout.

Although each meter is slightly different, here are some general guidelines for using your meter:

1. Make sure your hands are clean before you test.
2. Use a new lancet for each finger stick; follow instructions for how much blood you need for your test strip to work correctly. Some meters are certified to read blood

samples from alternative sites—so you can give your fingertips a rest.

3. Record all results.

4. For detailed information and problem-solving tips, refer to the manual for the meter you are using. Use the manufacturer's toll-free number for technical help whenever you need it.

Keeping It Accurate

The basic accuracy of your test results starts with the quality of the meter and the test strips that you use—and how you use them. But other factors can interfere as well. For example, altitude, temperature, and humidity indoors and out can cause unpredictable results. Careful storing and handling of the meter and test strips may ease the problem; ask your manufacturer for tips on how to handle these potential disruptions. You may also run into trouble if you use test strips that are not recommended by the manufacturer for your particular machine. Sometimes a company makes changes to its test strips, but the manufacturers of generic brands don't follow suit.

You can also have problems with the accuracy of your meter readings if you have certain health issues: for example, people with sickle cell anemia and anemia may have abnormal hemocrit levels (the amount of red blood cells in the blood). This alters the glucose readings. Elevated uric acid, or the presence of glutathione or vitamin C, can also change readings. Talk to your doctor about these potential problems.

F. Insulin Information

There are four types of insulin: rapid, regular, intermediate, and long-acting. Some come premixed; the most common mix is 70 percent NPH and 30 percent regular. NPH stands for Neutral Protamine Hagedora and is an intermediate-acting insulin.

Rapid insulin starts working about fifteen minutes after injection and continues to be effective for two to four hours with a peak at about one to two hours. Available by prescription only, it is sold as Humalog insulin lispro injection, NovoLog insulin aspart injection, or Apidra insulin glulisine injection. All three are clear.

Regular, or short-acting, human insulin reaches the bloodstream in about a half an hour and has an effect that peaks at two to three hours and is effective for around three to six hours depending on the person, their diet, and their level of physical activity. It is sold as Humulin R or Novolin R. They are also clear.

Intermediate, or NPH, insulin hits the blood after about two to four hours, peaks from four to ten hours, and may be effective for ten to sixteen hours. It is sold as Humulin N or Novolin N.

Long-acting insulins do not have peaks but hum along in the bloodstream, mimicking the way the body provides a sustained base level of insulin. There are two: Insulin glargine, sold as Lantus, is a clear liquid that kicks in after two to four hours and cannot be mixed with any other type of insulin. It can be taken any time of the day as long as it is that same time every day. Its duration is twenty to twenty-four hours. Insulin detemir, sold as Levemir, has an onset after one to two hours and lasts up to twenty-four hours. It is also clear and cannot be used in insulin pumps.

Traditionally, people with type 1 have taken only insulin, but new studies show that in some circumstances oral diabetes medication (usually taken by those with type 2 diabetes) may help. For example, recent studies suggest that a drug called metformin might help people with type 1 diabetes who are overweight, are receiving large doses of insulin, or have an A1C of higher than 8 percent. That is because they seem to have insulin resistance—and that may make their injections less effective. Any person with diabetes who develops ketones must stop metformin immediately because of rare but serious side effects.

G. Simplifying Complications

It's important for people to understand the risks and the results of all the various health problems that diabetes can trigger. They include cardiovascular disease—problems with the macro, or large, blood vessels, which can lead to heart attack and stroke—and diseases associated with the micro, or small, blood vessels, such as kidney, nerve, and eye disease. And there are others, as wide-ranging as dental problems and emotional disturbances, that also are associated with both type 1 and type 2 diabetes. Interestingly, not all of our internal organs and systems are negatively affected by the constant bath of high glucose levels, just the ones that do not have the ability to shut out glucose from the cells if it gets too high. The liver can do that, so it is not damaged by diabetes. But the retina cannot, perhaps because it needs a lot of glucose to do its job.

Whatever the reasons, it hardly seems fair that in addition to the daily peril that comes from simply not having enough insulin to survive, diabetics have to contend with these other health issues, but it's important to face them head-on, because—thank heavens—they can be avoided or diminished and treated very effectively. John Lachin, a principal investigator for the Diabetes Control and Complications Trial (DCCT) follow-up study of the Epidemiology of Diabetes Interventions and Complications (EDIC), as well as coprincipal investigator for the Diabetes Prevention Program (DPP), has boiled down the basic processes that lead to complications.

"For years people didn't really know how elevated glucose levels lead to complications—they thought it might be a short-acting phenomenon. But we know now, from looking at long-term studies such as the DCCT, that the damage takes years to show up, and even if you get your glucose levels under control, the cascade of chemical changes in the body that is set in motion by episodes of high blood sugar early on causes damage to cells throughout the body."

This damage comes in the form of what is called oxidative stress (that's from those free radicals that we are always saying antioxidants can help tame) and glycolization (attachment of sugars to cells that line the blood vessels that makes them inflexible and plaque-attracting so they get narrow). And that causes micro- and probably macrovascular damage.

Adds Michael Brownlee, who holds the Anita and Jack Saltz Chair of Diabetes Research at the Albert Einstein College of Medicine in New York, "The free radicals that are produced as a result of hyperglycemia are the underlying cause for most complications."

Heart Disease and Stroke

- Heart disease and stroke account for about 65 percent of deaths in people with diabetes.
- Adults with diabetes have heart disease death rates about two to four times higher than adults without diabetes.
- The risk for stroke is two to four times higher among people with diabetes.
- The good news, and there is always good news somewhere, says Dr. Brownlee, is that "we know that statins can really lower the damaging kind of cholesterol and actually reverse some of the atherosclerosis."

High Blood Pressure

- About 73 percent of adults with diabetes have blood pressure greater than or equal to the recommended good target level of 130/80, or they have lowered it through the use of prescription medication.
- Hypertension plays a role in causing kidney disease and, as kidney disease progresses, physical changes in the kidneys lead to increased blood pressure.
- Early detection and treatment of even mild hypertension is essential for people with diabetes.

Blindness

- Diabetes is the leading cause of new cases of blindness among adults aged twenty to seventy-four years.
- Diabetic retinopathy causes 12,000 to 24,000 new cases of blindness each year.

Kidney Disease

- Diabetes is the leading cause of kidney failure, accounting for 44 percent of new cases in 2002.
- In 2002 in the United States and Puerto Rico, 153,730 people with end-stage kidney disease due to diabetes were living on chronic dialysis or with a kidney transplant.

Nervous System Disease

- About 60 to 70 percent of people with diabetes have mild to severe forms of diabetes-related nerve damage. It can cause lack of feeling in hands and feet, slowed digestion of food in the stomach (called gastroparesis), and carpal tunnel syndrome. Severe forms of diabetic nerve disease are a major contributing cause of lower-extremity amputations.

Amputations

- In 2002, about 82,000 nontraumatic lower-limb amputations were performed in people with diabetes.

Dental Disease

- Periodontal (gum) disease is more common in people with diabetes. Among young adults, those with diabetes have about twice the risk of those without diabetes—and almost a third have advanced gum disease.

Other Complications

- Uncontrolled diabetes often leads to biochemical imbalances that can cause acute, life-threatening events, such as diabetic coma. In addition, people with diabetes are more susceptible to many other illnesses, including the flu, and once they acquire these illnesses, often have worse prognoses.

H. Foot Care

Taking care of your feet is not trivial—if you don't, the results can be very serious. But the good news is that infection and amputation—the two end results of neglected foot health—can be almost entirely avoided if you are absolutely conscientious about those tootsies. This is an issue for people with diabetes because we tend to have poor circulation in our extremities—that means that we are slow to heal from even the slightest scratches or wounds—have high blood sugar levels that seem to encourage bacterial growth, and have nerve damage that makes it difficult to feel a wound, even a severe one. In addition, nerve damage can cause hammertoes (as can too-short shoes). With hammertoes and short shoes, your toes curl under and you may get sores on the bottoms of your feet and on the tops of your toes. If this is happening to your feet, talk to your doctor about the best shoes and self-care routine to avoid injury.

Around 15 percent of people with diabetes develop foot ulcers, and there were more than 82,000 diabetes-related amputations in 2002. But, according to Daniel Einhorn, M.D., F.A.C.E., and secretary of the board of directors of the American Association of Clinical Endocrinologists, comprehensive foot-care programs can reduce amputations by 45 to 85 percent. And peripheral bypass graft surgery, which takes a vein from the patient's leg and uses it to form a new artery, can prevent amputation in a vast number of cases of serious infection by restoring circulation to affected areas so the injury can heal. Once more I'm in awe of doctors who can transform what at first seems silly and then serious into a manageable medical event.

So here's a simple six-step plan to make sure you are still stepping. . . .

1. Wash your feet in warm, not hot, water every day. Don't soak them, and dry them very well, especially between the toes.
2. Visually inspect them after you wash them. If you cannot see the bottoms of your feet and between your toes, use a mirror made for that purpose or have someone else do the inspection.
3. Rub lotion on dry skin, but not between the toes.
4. If you have corns or calluses, very gently file them with an emery board after your bath or shower.
5. Cut your toenails as needed; file edges using an emery board.
6. Don't go barefoot, even indoors. And always wear socks or stockings when you wear shoes to help protect your feet from blisters. Make sure the elastic top to the socks does not reduce your circulation.

I. Glaucoma

In addition to retinopathy, diabetes is associated with two other eye problems—cataracts and glaucoma. People with diabetes get them more often and at younger ages. A yearly visit to an ophthalmologist to check for these and other problems is essential.

There are two main types of glaucoma. The more common is primary open-angle glaucoma (POAG), in which fluid drains too slowly from the eye and causes a chronic rise in eye pressure. Type 2 diabetes is associated with POAG. The other kind of glaucoma is called closed angle. It happens because the iris drops over the point where it meets the white covering over the eye (sclera) and where fluid within the inner eye drains. When this blockage happens, the pressure inside the eye can rise very quickly and cause eye pain and redness; decreased vision; colored halos; headaches; and nausea and vomiting. I was aware of none of these symptoms.

Because raised eye pressure can damage the optic nerve and lead to vision loss, a closed-angle glaucoma attack must be treated immediately. Using a laser, a small hole is made in the iris to create a new pathway for the aqueous fluid to drain from the eye. The surgery is performed on an outpatient basis, usually in the doctor's office. The actual procedure takes but a few minutes.

J. Diabetes and Depression

According to the National Diabetes Education Program, recent studies have shown that people with diabetes have a higher risk of developing depression, and that adults with depression are 37 percent more likely to develop type 2 diabetes. Among people with type 1, the incidence of depression seems to correlate with the development of complications—those who are healthy suffer from depression at the same rate as nondiabetics.

Currently, only 30 percent of people diagnosed with depression and diabetes receive adequate treatment for depression, yet treatment can make it easier to control glucose levels, to exercise, and to follow a doctor's suggested medication routine.

K. Amazing Insights

We are moving ever closer to untangling the genetic forces that put people at risk for type 1 and type 2 diabetes, to understanding the causes of complications associated with it, and to finding ever-smarter ways to manage and even prevent the disease. Here's a list of some of the most promising research efforts at the time the book was completed. (Some even more amazing ones may arise, and some of these may not pan out. That is always the chance that investigators take.) It is important for everyone with diabetes to be aware of just what powerful forces are at work in the search for a cure. Here's what Richard A. Insel, M.D., Executive Vice President of Research at the Juvenile Diabetes Research Foundation, suggested as projects that are focusing on major areas of research over the next five years:

1. first-generation closed-loop artificial pancreas being evaluated in the clinic
2. performance of successful proof-of-concept clinical trials of beta cell regeneration therapeutics

3. development of a replenishable, functional, alternative beta cell source for replacement

4. development of immunotherapeutics that arrest onset and progression of type 1 diabetes

5. development of therapeutics that arrest progression and partially reverse diabetic eye disease

Early Detection

Not only have researchers found a new antibody that confers a 96 percent certainty that the person with it will go on to develop type 1, but they have now identified a sign of inflammation that arises before any antibodies can be detected at all. Researchers at the Medical College of Wisconsin have found what they call a proinflammatory signature—the presence of certain proteins and cellular molecules that tell the immune system to take action—in this case, leading to the destruction of the beta cells.

Why does this matter? Using a simple blood test, doctors may be able to intervene in the cascade of events that lead up to full-blown diabetes. And the earlier they can step in, the more likely they are to be able to preserve beta cell function and prevent the death of a critical number of beta cells.

Islets in Action

Islet cell transplantation is one of the most difficult yet most promising routes to controlling diabetes. But researchers are battling a host of obstacles, not the least of which is the fact that once the cells are put into an individual, many of them seem to fail. Now, according to researchers at the University of Miami Miller School of Medicine and at the Karolinska

Institutet in Stockholm, Sweden, doctors may be able to learn what happens to those transplanted cells once they enter the body. Using a sophisticated form of photon microscope, called multiphoton confocal microscopy technology, it's as if they "were observing the transplants through a window in real time," says Camillo Ricordi, M.D., Scientific Director of the University of Miami's Diabetes Research Institute. "It lets us follow biological processes, like the effect of a novel intervention, for example. One of the biggest problems with islet cell transplantation has been having enough of the insulin-producing cells survive the transplant process itself; now we have a window into that living world and this will expedite research considerably."

CD3

Several efforts to engineer a so-called monoclonal anti-CD3 antibody that will stop the immune system from killing off the beta cells are showing enormous promise. JDRF-funded research allowed MacroGenics' anti-CD3 compound teplizumab and Tolerx's anti-CD3 compound otelixizumab to proceed to advanced clinical trials in partnership with Eli Lilly and GSK, respectively.

One such study, called Protégé, uses teplizumab. In a joint project with JDRF, scientists are exploring its effectiveness. "Anti-CD3 treatment is one of a few approaches shown to change the clinical course of new-onset type 1 diabetes," said Dr. Insel. Since the treatment keeps the beta cells alive and pumping out insulin, the theory is that it reduces the amount of insulin a person needs to take, makes it easier to keep glucose levels near normal, and may reduce diabetes-related

complications. Another such JDRF-supported effort is the DE-
FEND trial. A phase III study of otelixizumab in new-onset
type 1 diabetes will determine if the FDA approves the drug for
use or not. This trial will evaluate whether a single course of
otelixizumab is able to stop beta cell death and reduce the
amount of insulin needed by the newly diagnosed.

L. Stem Cells

JDRF was a founder of the Coalition for the Advancement of
Medical Research (CAMR), a diverse coalition of health-
related organizations committed to sustaining federal funding
of stem cell research. Working through CAMR and indepen-
dently, JDRF volunteers and staff played a crucial role in 2001
in convincing the George W. Bush administration and con-
gressional leadership not to support a total ban on embryonic
stem cell research in the United States. More recently, JDRF
worked to build bipartisan support for passage of H.R. 810—
The Castle-DeGette Stem Cell Research Enhancement Act
of 2005. JDRFers were also lead proponents of California's
newly enacted $3 billion stem cell research/regenerative med-
icine initiative.

The experience of the JDRF along with the HIV and AIDS
community, the women's health movement, the Parkinson's Action Network, and other grassroots organizations proves that in
their quests to find a cure for their children and loved ones for
whatever pains them, moms and dads, partners and spouses, and
all people who care will never give up. In fact, people personally

affected by illness are the natural and necessary leaders of any global cure movement. They understand the urgency and are uniquely willing do anything required to ensure that their loved ones are freed of the burden of disease as soon as possible. For them, "failure is not an option," because their very survival is at stake.

For people with type 1 diabetes, we look first to stem cell research as a means to help us replace the insulin-producing cells of the pancreas that are destroyed by our disease. However, it also may provide insights into the genetic basis of diabetes, including the differences between type 1 diabetes, which is an autoimmune disease like lupus and multiple sclerosis, and the more common, obesity-related type 2 diabetes. It may also provide solutions to the devastating complications of diabetes: blindness, kidney failure, amputation, and cardiovascular disease. For people with Parkinson's disease, stem cell research holds the promise of replacing destroyed specialized brain cells and thereby freeing patients from the prison of disease-induced rigidity. For spinal injury patients, it offers the potential for regeneration of neural tissue, which would reconnect the pathways of sensation and motor control and allow them to walk again, or talk again, or hug their child again. For people with heart failure, stem cell research may mean sleeping through the night without a struggle for breath, dancing with a spouse, working in the garden, or sustaining one's job and independence. For the person with macular degeneration it might offer sight.

Stem cell research offers hope for people with a great diversity of illnesses, for people of all ages, genders, and backgrounds.

M. The Continuous Glucose Monitor/ Artificial Pancreas

I don't want to leave you with a bad impression of the amazing scientific effort that is being put into the CGM and insulin pump hookup: The extraordinary goal is an artificial pancreas that even stum-bumblers like me can use. Researchers are working to create the yet-to-be-perfected artificial pancreas by combining an insulin pump with a continuous glucose monitor (CGM) and a transmitter that allows them to communicate. This will make a closed-loop system that is self-regulating and secretes insulin in response to a person's changing glucose levels, just like a body without diabetes does. The goal is to counter glucose highs and lows and maintain levels in the normal range. This is vital because a 2005 study revealed that even the most conscientious people who check blood glucose frequently spend less than 30 percent of the day in the normal glucose range.

Some experts, such as Yale's Dr. William Tamborlane, who developed the first insulin pump in 1978, believe that a slightly "less than closed" loop system, in which the user still evaluates readings, particularly before meals, and makes insulin dosing decisions when needed, is a more realistic goal. But whatever the future brings, it promises to make a dramatic improvement in people's ability to stabilize their glucose levels.

JDRF has a major commitment to the creation of a closed-loop system and has established the JDRF Artificial Pancreas Project. One of the centers that they fund, the Yale–New Haven Children's Hospital, released the first results of a clinical trial of the system on adolescents. According to the hospital, "In a trial with seventeen teenagers, who agreed to spend three days in the hospital testing the device, YNHCH researchers found the artificial pancreas achieved a level of glucose control that was far superior to methods subjects had used previously. Even though these youngsters had very good A1C's at home on a pump, they still saw vast improvement when they used the closed-loop system. At home the glucose levels were held in the range of 70 to 180 only 58 percent of the day; on the closed-loop system they were in that range 82 percent of the time. This is because the device achieved near-normal glucose control at night, when dangerous dips and surges in blood sugar are difficult to monitor and patients risk serious hyperglycemic episodes. Researchers also reported improved glucose levels after meals, another period of serious fluctuations, when they added user-controlled manual 'priming' doses of insulin before meals."

"I would say the 'artificial pancreas' is not really a cure for diabetes, but it's a bridge to a cure that will vastly improve the quality of life for people with type 1 diabetes," said Stuart Alan Weinzimer, M.D., attending pediatric endocrinologist at YNHCH, associate professor at the Yale School of Medicine, and lead author of the study. "In the next five years, it's going to change the face of diabetes treatment by leaps and bounds. Everything that most pediatricians have learned about diabetes management is going to go completely out the window."

Yale used a Medtronic continuous glucose monitor. DexCom and Abbott Laboratories also make FDA-approved continuous glucose monitors (CGM); others are in the works.

The CGMs use a sensor inserted just under the skin that monitors glucose levels continuously (it must be changed every three to seven days). The readings show up on a monitor screen. When it is part of the closed-loop system it has a wireless transmitter that uses a computer algorithm to tell the insulin pump how to regulate the delivery of insulin based on information from the sensor. The main stumbling block to the closed-loop system, according to JDRF's Aaron Kowalski, Ph.D., Director of Strategic Research Projects and an enthusiastic CGM user, is to make sure that the algorithm is flawless and there is no risk of delivering too much insulin. "The continuous sensors themselves are fantastic," he says. "I have been using it for about two years, and my brother, who was diagnosed with type 1 diabetes when he was three, and has suffered from terrible blood sugar problems for more than thirty years, is using it now and it is a godsend. But while his lows have been reduced, they have not been eliminated."

That, says Kowalski, is because of the very nature of contending with type 1 diabetes. "There are two challenges that everyone with diabetes faces: keeping glucose levels under control and maintaining mental balance. Diabetes is stressful, hard to deal with, constant—it never goes away. The CGM helps people do better with glucose control, but it makes the stress of managing diabetes even more intense for some people. You see the device and its readout all the time, it is right in front of you and it's beeping and beeping. People cannot necessarily cope with that all the time. Once you make the CGM part of the closed-loop system, however, it will regulate glucose levels better, and become less intrusive, demand far less attention."

Refinements to the closed-loop system that are being explored include experimental insulin pumps that have been modified to give microdoses. "These experimental pumps administer microdoses every few minutes, instead of a basal dose," explains Kowalski. "We have tried this in controlled hospital settings and the results overall are fantastic." Researchers at a JDRF-funded project at Harvard and Boston University are also experimenting on pigs—and now in humans—with devices that deliver both insulin and glucagon. "That's the brake and the accelerator," says Kowalski.

All of these refinements may help overcome an intrinsic difference between the bodies of people with and without diabetes. "When people without diabetes sit down at a table and look at a menu or start thinking about eating, they are hard-wired to prime their body to start secreting insulin," explains Kowalski. "So when a person without diabetes eats, their insulin peaks in about fifteen or twenty minutes. That doesn't happen in a person with diabetes; it takes about two hours after they give themselves an injection. To get a fully closed loop is very, very challenging using today's insulins. You might need a faster-acting insulin or another way to get it into the body. But even with the insulin we have, you can get someone significantly better—A1C's in the low 6's or upper 5's—without any lows! And that means there is significantly less of a burden on the person with diabetes and his or her family."

N. Getting Control

There has been some debate about the pros and cons of intensive glucose control. One major study, called the ACCORD

Trial, put some people with type 2 diabetes, who also had heart disease or at least two risk factors for it, on a strict routine designed to lower their cholesterol and/or high blood pressure and keep their A1C at 6 or below (a full point below the current recommendations). Some of the people who were in the intensive A1C control group had a higher death rate from cardiovascular events than those on a regimen aimed at A1C's of 7 to 7.9. Did this mean that tight control was dangerous across the board? Absolutely not.

John Lachin is a professor of biostatistics and epidemiology at The George Washington University. Knowledge about preventing and treating diabetes has taken great strides forward as a result of his decades-long involvement with a series of NIH-funded trials. He is currently a principal investigator for the DCCT follow-up study of the Epidemiology of Diabetes Interventions and Complications (EDIC), as well as co–principal investigator for the Diabetes Prevention Program (DPP). "Type 1 and 2 diabetes are two entirely different diseases with entirely different pathophysiology. In type 1, the data are definitive that lower A1C is better. But other factors may be operating in type 2. Basically we know that for people who have either type 1 or type 2 diabetes an A1C of about seven has enormous benefits."

In the follow-up Epidemiology of Diabetes Interventions and Complications study, the DCCT participants who maintained strict control saw their incidence of cardiovascular disease cut by more than 50 percent compared to those who had not maintained tight control. "The longer we follow patients, the more we're impressed by the lasting benefits of tight glucose control," says Saul Genuth, M.D., of Case Western Reserve

University in Cleveland. Dr. Genuth chairs the EDIC study. "Intensive glucose control significantly reduces heart disease as well as damage to the eyes, nerves, and kidneys of people with type 1 diabetes."

O. The Lowdown on Low Blood Sugar

Hypoglycemia, also called low blood sugar, happens when your blood glucose (blood sugar) level drops too low to provide fuel to your body's cells. You get glucose into your bloodstream from carbohydrates that you eat: rice, bread, cereal, fruits, sugary and sweet foods, milk, pasta, flour, and grains. Insulin, secreted by beta cells in folks without diabetes, or from an injection if you have type 1 (or sometimes type 2), is a hormone that unlocks the door to the cell and allows glucose to travel from the bloodstream into the cell. In people without diabetes, insulin level is determined by food intake and the blood glucose level, allowing a match between supply and demand of glucose to balance out high levels of glucose and keep blood sugar levels steady. If someone without diabetes eats more glucose than their body needs, their blood sugar never gets high. Instead the sugar is stored in the liver and muscles as a form that can be quickly accessed—glycogen. The body can use the stored glucose whenever it is needed for energy between meals. Extra glucose can also be converted to fat and stored in fat cells.

Glucose levels may become low when, for example, you exercise a lot or skip a meal. When that happens, in theory, glucagon, another hormone produced by the pancreas, signals the liver to break down glycogen and release glucose, hopefully restoring a normal glucose level. But people with diabetes may miscalculate their insulin need and take more than they need—which can send levels too low, or they may exercise more than they expected to and not eat sufficient carbohydrates to compensate, or they may simply have unstable glucose levels that unpredictably seem to dip, perhaps while they sleep, causing night sweats, nightmares, or confusion. We also now know that type 1-ers often have an impaired glucagon response. In fact, the DCCT findings indicate that we're wrong to assume hypoglycemia is usually triggered by not eating enough, taking too much insulin, or getting too much exercise. In the study, most incidences of hypoglycemia didn't happen for those reasons, indicating that low blood sugars may strike because those with type 1 have a basic defect in the body's ability to regulate glucose levels.

Common symptoms of hypoglycemia include nervousness, shakiness, dizziness, confusion, anxiety, and tiredness.

Prevention

Frequent glucose testing, testing before (and during) exercise, the use of a monitor that indicates glucose level trends (and alerts you when you are headed up or down), sticking to your medication routine and paying attention to what and when you eat, and adjusting your insulin as needed—all these steps can help you prevent low blood sugar. But sometimes despite your best efforts, for reasons you cannot figure out, you will go low. Don't beat yourself up about it. The important thing is to take the right steps to bring it up quickly and safely. The National Institute of Diabetes and Digestive and Kidney Diseases suggests that a reading of 70 mg/dL or lower calls for a quick-fix food right away. Options include:

- 2 or 3 glucose tablets
- ½ cup (4 ounces) of any fruit juice
- ½ cup (4 ounces) of a regular (not diet) soft drink
- 1 cup (8 ounces) of milk
- 5 or 6 pieces of hard candy
- 1 or 2 teaspoons of sugar or honey

They then recommend that you wait fifteen minutes and check your blood glucose level again. If it is still too low, have another one of the quick-fix foods listed above. Repeat these steps until your blood glucose is at least 70. Then, if it will be an hour or more before your next meal, have a snack.

If you lose consciousness or cannot eat or do not catch the low until it has plummeted, glucagon can be injected to quickly raise your blood glucose level. You should always have a glucagon kit at home and at work; children should give them to their school nurse. You should also teach family, friends, and school staff how and when to give a glucagon injection. Any time glucagon is given, an ambulance should be called.

Talk to your doctor about any severe low blood sugar requiring assistance of others for recovery or glucagon use, so you can adjust your medication and nutritional routine.

P. Carb Counting

For many type 1 diabetics, knowing the carbohydrate content of the food they eat is something they do without question every time they put any food into their system. They rely on computerized carb counters, nutritional labels on packaged foods, carbohydrate exchange lists, what they have memorized over time, and intuition—all balanced with conscientious glucose monitoring before and after they eat. It gives them the most freedom to eat what they want and adjust their insulin to keep in good control.

The amount of carbohydrates you eat in a day should be determined through discussions with your doctor, nutritionist, and diabetes educator, but on a 2,000-calorie-a-day meal plan you may take in up to half of your calories from carbohydrates, according to the NIDDK.

One serving (approximately 15 grams of carbohydrates) =

1	slice bread
⅓	cup cooked rice
¾	cup dry, unsweetened cereal
¼	bagel
½	cup cooked pasta
1	medium sugar cookie
1	cup milk
1½	cups cooked broccoli
3	cups fresh lettuce
4	ounces of juice or soda

1   small piece (or 1 cup) of fresh fruit

⅓   cup cooked beans, peas, or lentils

½   cup mashed potatoes

3   cups popcorn

¼   cup granola

⅓   cup hummus

Q. The Skin You're In

The skin is the largest organ in the body—and it's little wonder that diabetes can affect it, just as it does other organs. First, high glucose levels can make your body lose fluids, which dries out the skin. When that happens the skin is more vulnerable to becoming itchy, cracked, and infected. This may create slow-healing wounds, and that, in its extreme, can lead to amputation.

Diabetes can also affect your skin as a result of nerve damage or neuropathy. When nerves don't function properly (you lose feeling in your legs, feet, or hands, for example), those areas stop being able to produce sweat in sufficient quantities to keep skin soft and moist. To avoid these problems, control your blood sugars, drink lots of water, and use nonirritating moisturizers after every bath or shower and during the day, if needed. See your doctor immediately about all skin sores or wounds, before they become chronic.

Other skin problems that affect people with type 2 as well as those with type 1 diabetes include:

- bacterial infections that are known as sties (in the eyelid glands), boils (in hair follicles), and carbuncles (in the skin and tissue underneath)
- fungal infections, particularly yeast infections

Diabetes Resource Guide

Juvenile Diabetes Research Foundation International (JDRF)
120 Wall Street
New York, NY 10005-4001
Phone: 800-533-CURE (2873)
Fax: 212-785-9595
E-mail: info@jdrf.org
Internet: www.jdrf.org
Publications available include:

Countdown Magazine: Read in-depth analyses of cutting-edge diabetes research and treatments, profiles, and more.

Countdown for Kids: Check out the first magazine especially for kids with diabetes; information, fun, role models, pen pals.

Research E-Newsletter: Get the latest information about research on type 1 diabetes and its complications.

Emerging Technologies in Diabetes Research E-Newsletter: Follow the progress of JDRF's Artificial Pancreas Project and other technological advances in diabetes research.

Life with Diabetes E-Newsletter: Get important information on diabetes management, nutrition, exercise, technology, and more.

Books: Browse a selection of current books to help you live with diabetes.

American Diabetes Association (ADA)

For information about type 1 and type 2 diabetes, recipes, publications, research updates, and more.

1701 North Beauregard Street

Alexandria, VA 22311

Phone: 800-DIABETES (800-342-2383) (National Call Center)

703-549-1500 (National Service Center)

800-232-3472 (professional member department only)

Fax: 703-549-6995

E-mail: askada@diabetes.org

Internet: www.diabetes.org

The trained staff at 800-DIABETES is dedicated to answering thousands of calls and e-mails. Monday through Friday from 8:30 A.M. to 8:00 P.M. EST.

American Association of Diabetes Educators

A certified diabetes educator can help you when you are first diagnosed, or work with you to improve your diabetes control at any point, even years after diagnosis. They will collaborate with your doctor to offer you techniques for improving compliance, nutrition and exercise routines, and tips for lowering your A1C.

To find a diabetes educator in your area, visit www.diabetese ducator.org/DiabetesEducation/Find.html.

American Dietetic Association (ADA)

For food and nutrition information and a complete diabetes exchange list.

120 South Riverside Plaza, Suite 2000
Chicago, IL 60606-6995
Phone: 800-877-1600 or 800-877-0877
800-877-1600, ext. 5000 (referral to registered dieticians)
Fax: 312-899-4899
E-mail: knowledge@eatright.org
Internet: www.eatright.org

Diabetes Exercise and Sports Association (DESA)

For $20 a year you can become a member and receive information on diet/nutrition and exercise; particularly useful for people taking insulin.

10216 Taylorsville Road, Suite 900
Louisville, KY 40299
Phone: 800-898-4322
Fax: 502-261-8346
E-mail: desa@diabetes-exercise.org
Internet: www.diabetes-exercise.org

Centers for Disease Control and Prevention

National Center for Chronic Disease Prevention and Health Promotion
Division of Diabetes Translation
Mail Stop K-10
4770 Buford Highway, NE
Atlanta, GA 30341-3717

Phone: 770-448-5000 or 800-CDC-INFO (800-232-4636)
TTY: 888-232-6348
Fax: 770-488-5966
E-mail: diabetes@cdc.gov
Internet: www.cdc.gov/diabetes

Diabetes Public Health Resource
www.cdc.gov/diabetes

Diabetes and Me
www.cdc.gov/diabetes/consumer/index.htm

Online publications
www.cdc.gov/diabetes/pubs/online.htm

National Institute of Diabetes and Digestive and Kidney Diseases (NIDDK)

Internet: www.niddk.nih.gov
This is the government's lead agency for diabetes research. The NIDDK operates three information clearinghouses of potential interest to people seeking diabetes information and funds six diabetes research and training centers and eight diabetes endocrinology research centers.
Introduction to Diabetes
http://diabetes.niddk.nih.gov/intro/

For Spanish-language information:
http://diabetes.niddk.nih.gov/index_sp.htm

National Diabetes Information Clearinghouse
1 Information Way
Bethesda, MD 20892-3560
Phone: 800-860-8747
Fax: 703-738-4929
E-mail: ndic@info.niddk.nih.gov
Internet: www.diabetes.niddk.nih.gov
For an A-to-Z listing of topics and titles, information for the newly diagnosed, details on treatments and diabetes-related complications, statistics, online publications, and more. All information is also available in Spanish.

National Diabetes Education Program
1 Diabetes Way
Bethesda, MD 20814-9692
Phone: 888-693-NDEP (888-693-6337)
Fax: 703-738-4929
E-mail: ndep@mail.nih.gov
Internet: www.ndep.nih.gov
www.ndep.nih.gov/diabetes/pubs/catalog.htm#PubsPatCont
Publications for consumers in a variety of languages, including English, Spanish, Cambodian, Tagalog, Thai, Chinese, Korean, Tongan, Vietnamese, and Samoan.

For information on working with your school to set up a good program for managing your child's diabetes:
www.ndep.nih.gov/resources/school.htm

For information pertaining to children and adolescents' management of diabetes: www.ndep.nih.gov/diabetes/youth/youth_ResDirectory.htm

Weight-Control Information Network (WIN)

1 WIN Way

Bethesda, MD 20892-3665

Phone: 877-946-4627 or 202-828-1025

Fax: 202-828-1028

E-mail: win@info.niddk.nih.gov

Internet: http://win.niddk.nih.gov

Part of the NIDDK, this site offers nutritional guidance and information on safe and effective weight management.

American Association of Clinical Endocrinologists (AACE)

1245 Riverside Avenue, Suite 200

Jacksonville, FL 32202

Phone: 904-353-7878

Fax: 904-353-8185

Internet: www.aace.com

For information on how to find an endocrinologist who specializes in diabetes in your locale.

U.S. Food and Drug Administration Diabetes Information

On insulins: www.fda.gov/diabetes/insulin.html

On glucose monitors: www.fda.gov/diabetes/glucose.html

On oral diabetes medications: www.fda.gov/diabetes/pills.html

On complications of diabetes: www.fda.gov/diabetes/related.html

Complication-Related Information

National Kidney Disease Education Program (NKDEP)
3 Kidney Information Way
Bethesda, MD 20892
Phone: 866-4-KIDNEY or 866-454-3639
Fax: 301-402-8182
E-mail: nkdep@info.niddk.nih.gov
Internet: www.nkdep.nih.gov

National Eye Institute (NEI)
2020 Vision Place
Bethesda, MD 20892-3655
Phone: 800-869-2020 (for health professionals only)
Fax: 301-402-1065
E-mail: 2020@nei.nih.gov
Internet: www.nei.nih.gov

National Heart Lung and Blood Institute (NHLBI) Information Center
P.O. Box 30105
Bethesda, MD 20824-0105
Phone: 301-592-8573
TTY: 240-629-3255
Fax: 240-629-3246
E-mail: nhlbiinfo@nhlbi.nih.gov
Internet: www.nhlbi.nih.gov

**National Institute of Dental and Craniofacial Research/
National Oral Health Information Clearinghouse
(NOHIC)**
1 NOHIC Way
Bethesda, MD 20892-3500
Phone: 301-402-7364
Fax: 301-480-4098
E-mail: nidcrinfo@mail.nih.gov
Internet: www.nidcr.nih.gov

American Podiatric Medical Association (APMA)
9312 Old Georgetown Road
Bethesda, MD 20814-1621
Phone: 301-581-9200
Fax: 301-530-2752
Internet: www.apma.org

APMA Foot Care Information Center
Phone: 800-FOOT-CARE (800-366-8227)

American Urological Association (AUA)
1000 Corporate Boulevard, Suite 410
Linthicum, MD 21090
Phone: 866-RINGAUA (866-746-4282) or 410-689-3700
Fax: 410-689-3800
E-mail: aua@auanet.org
Internet: www.auanet.org

National Kidney Foundation, Inc. (NKF)
30 East 33rd Street
New York, NY 10016
Phone: 800-622-9010 or 212-889-2210
Fax: 212-689-9261
E-mail: info@kidney.org
Internet: www.kidney.org

Index